STAGE LIGHTING DESIGN

A Practical Guide

Neil Fraser

with a Foreword by Richard Attenborough

The Crowood Press

First published in 1999 by
The Crowood Press Ltd
Ramsbury, Marlborough
Wiltshire SN8 2HR

www.crowood.com

This impression 2007

**British Library Cataloguing-in-Publication
Data**
A catalogue record for this book is available from
the British Library.

ISBN 978 1 86126 248 6

Photographic Acknowledgements
All photographs are by the author except:
Page 7 Richard Attenborough Productions. Figs 3,
34 (top left), 50 Leanne Archbold. Fig. 6 Sharlene
Whyte. Figs 7, 22, 24 CCT Lighting: Figs 15, 16,
87 (bottom) Strand Lighting. Fig. 25 Thomas
Engineering Ltd. Figs 46, 78 DHA Ltd. Figs 62,
88, 96–8, 131 Gary Thorne. Fig. 82 Le Maitre
Pyrotechnics. Fig. 87 (top) Vari*Lite UK. Fig. 127
Noriko Sakura. Fig. 129 New York Theatre
Exchange (Rania Calas).

Typefaces used: Photina (*headings and text*),
Book Antiqua (*boxed matter*).

Typeset and designed by
D & N Publishing
Membury Business Park
Lambourn Woodlands
Hungerford, Berkshire.

Printed and bound by GraphyCems

Dedication

This book is dedicated to my
children Alex and Holly, who are the
brightest of lights in my life.

Acknowledgements
Thank you to the companies and individuals who
have supplied or appeared in photographs, in particular Contact Theatre Co. in Manchester, Polka
Theatre for Children in Wimbledon, Liverpool Every-
man, Torch Theatre, Strand Lighting, CCT Lighting
Le Maitre Pyrotechnics, Vari*Lite UK. Thanks also to
Lord Attenborough and his staff, and all the staff and
students at the Royal Academy of Dramatic Art
(1985–present) – especially Gwen Tomson and Peter
Harrison for their help with the photographs, Leanne
Archbold for proofreading, help with diagrams, photographs, and general support, and to Kate Jones for
constant help and advice. Thanks also to Gary
Thorne and Shirley Matthews for their continuing
enthusiasm and encouragement.

CONTENTS

LIST OF EXERCISES

N.B. Key to lighting design plans is on page 50.

FOREWORD

by Richard Attenborough

I am enormously pleased to have been invited to introduce this book. Although it is a long time since I appeared in a theatre, I have never forgotten the vital importance of good lighting for the stage. Today, of course, I am keenly aware that this is also true of the medium of film

The allied professions of theatre and film, which have dominated my working life for nearly 60 years, are both immeasurably enhanced by the art of creating pictures. That is why the original term 'moving pictures', later shortened to 'movies', so aptly describes the cinema experience. Pictures, whether they be on stage or screen, tell stories and every story can be made – or marred – by the manner in which it is lit.

FOREWORD

Like good directors of photography, good stage lighting designers really do deserve to be fostered and encouraged. It seems to me that Neil Fraser's excellent book will do just this and that his text approaches the acquisition of professional lighting skills in exactly the right way.

As Chairman of RADA, where I trained as an actor during the War, I hold proper technical instruction in the highest possible esteem. At the Academy we quietly pride ourselves, not only in the contribution we make more famously to the world of acting, but also on the breadth of skilled technicians we have trained and sent out to become key members of the theatre profession.

RADA's courses in stage management and theatre production, in prop making, scenic construction and painting, wardrobe and costume making, and in stage lighting are all based on the same precepts which Neil Fraser, who has been Head of Lighting at the Academy Rada since 1985, has used throughout this book. They embody the idea that the vocational training requires the student to do, rather than just watch or listen. We are all aware that experiences made personal, made actual, are those from wich we really learn.

Neil's years of teaching at RADA and guest-lecturing throughout the world have helped him develop and refine the exercises which form the backbone of what follows. I believe you will find these exercises both imaginatively stimulating and of great practical use.

The theatre world can be hard at times, with long hours, low pay and poor funding, and yet it can also be one of the most wondrous, exciting and satisfying of professions. In making good use of this book and in realizing your own potential, I sincerely hope you will also take enormous pleasure in what you do.

So my very final enjoinder is that simple but all important word: enjoy!

INTRODUCTION

WHAT IS STAGE LIGHTING?

Any light source pointed at a darkened stage could be described as stage lighting. Any light aimed towards that dark, mysterious space will show something of what is there. Real stage lighting, however, does much more than this – it does not just illuminate an empty space.

Fig. 1 The beauty of light beams caught in smoke.

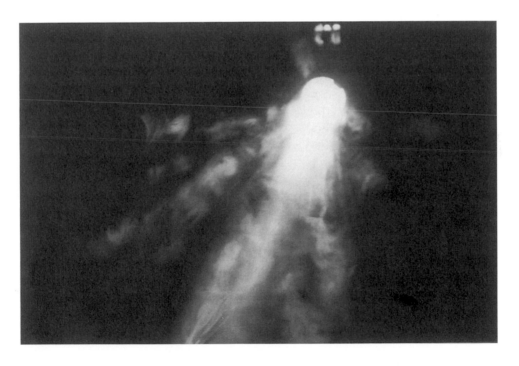

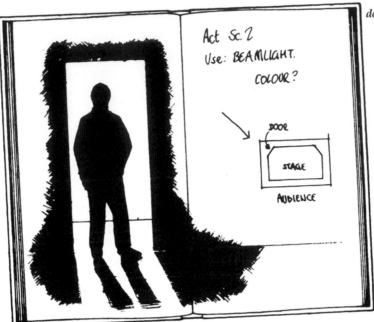

Fig. 2 A lighting designer's sketchbook.

Good stage lighting adds character to space, texture to object, emotion to event, impetus to action, and powerful dramatic emphasis to the stage picture. As would be expected, this takes time and practice to get right. *Stage Lighting Design* aims to accelerate this process and help you to become an accomplished stage lighting designer.

This book will help you to progress beyond gaining simple technical knowledge to develop good and varied techniques in the lighting of dramatic pieces for the stage. The world of stage lighting is introduced in such a way that skills will be developed at your own pace and in your own individual style. Alongside the development of good working methods you will also discover an overall personal design criteria – to not only 'do' lighting but also to 'think' lighting.

The book contains both comprehensive technical information and a wide range of practical exercises. Whilst the technical information stands in its own right, the exercises reinforce and develop the knowledge gained by making it personal to you. This will enable you to evolve an understanding of how light works within the artificial world of a stage space, to discover a means of interpreting this world to better interact with the art of the dramatist or director, and in doing so develop your own individual lighting style.

More than anything it is this individuality, supported by a good technical understanding, that creates good and unique lighting and makes a good lighting designer.

Certain instructional devices are used throughout the text. These are boxes, as illustrated below:

INFORMATION BOX

These boxes contain technical information immediately relevant to the area being discussed in the text.

SAFETY BOX

It is most important that at all times our work is safe. Safety Boxes are placed in the text specifically to warn the reader of any possible safety aspects that they may encounter.

A General Note on the Exercises

1. Each exercise is followed by an analysis of expected results. Do not be tempted to read the analysis of the exercise before carrying it out (unless advised to do so at some point in the exercise) – otherwise you are

SAFETY ISSUES

It is important to always seek advice if you are ever unsure about a safety issue whilst carrying out a practical exercise.

more likely to learn what the author thinks and not what you think!

2. In the case of those exercises in parts, carry out each part completely before moving on to the next one.
3. Think of and apply your own variations on the exercises – practice certainly makes perfect.
4. The exercises, as with the various sections of the book itself, are written to create a total guide to the world of lighting design. The starting point has to be that the reader knows nothing. Often this will not be the case and so you should either select the most relevant sections or exercises, or simply read through rather than carry out all the exercises.

FIRST AID

Everyone working in technical theatre work should be encouraged to have first aid training.

5. In some cases it is important to have other people look at your work. Often this is indicated in the exercise, but it is also important generally not to become too entrenched in your own ideas without reference to what others may think. Always be ready to share in this way and the results you achieve will be much enriched.

6. Further guidance on carrying out the exercises is to be found in the text.

7. If you intend to work through a number of exercises it may be a good idea to keep a written record of your journey through ideas. This may well then become a useful reference book in its own right as your career as a lighting designer or theatre technician progresses.

1

WHAT IS LIGHTING DESIGN?

'Seeing Is Believing'

LOOKING

Modern stage lighting is developed from an understanding of how light illuminates the real world around us. Seeing is, in essence, a simple task for most of us and not something that needs further description. However, lighting designers (often abbreviated to LD) need to be sure about what they see in the real world and how light 'works'. The first exercises in this book all deal with the need for lighting designers to be good at analysing the light around them.

EXERCISE 1
LOOKING AT LIGHT

Part 1

a. Go to a place where there is a strong light source, such as direct sunlight in a garden, strong sunlight coming through a window, or a desk lamp in an otherwise dark room.

b. Sit or stand in one place and look at any object in front of you.

c. Think of words to describe the way the light source is lighting what you see.

d. It may help to write down your impressions and to take a photograph for later reference.

Part 2

You should be able to answer many questions about what you are looking at, including:

✳ How many light sources are there?
✳ What part of the object is most brightly lit?
✳ Where do the shadows fall?
✳ Is anything in total darkness? Is any part of the object difficult to see clearly?
✳ Does the light on the object help it to blend in or stand out from the things around it?
✳ Do you like the way the light looks on the object? If so, why?
✳ Could you move your viewpoint and feel the light is being more effective?
✳ What do you mean by being more effective?

Repeat this exercise for another object in view and in a number of different locations, such as a cloudy garden, a room at night, a club, a library, or an office. Compare the way you have described each different situation.

Analysis – Exercise 1

What you see and what you learn from what you see in this exercise will depend very much on your chosen subject. Everybody will have different ideas and use different words to describe what they think they are seeing. What matters here is that you react honestly to what you see and do not start the exercise with any preconceived notions as to what you *think* you will see. To some extent the novice lighting designer needs to start to see the world afresh.

You should find as you repeat each exercise that the comparisons you make between them begin to give you a catalogue of references concerning which light source is brighter, which warmer, which more pleasant, which most successful at showing off an object, which not to your liking at all, and so on. The more you repeat this exercise as you go about your daily routine, the greater this

Fig. 3 Example for the analysis in Exercise 1.

catalogue of references will become, and you will become better at knowing and really *seeing* the effect light has on objects.

Example Analysis of Photograph in Fig. 3

* The sunlight gently crosses the scene from left to right.
* The trees are lit left side only, with some light crossing to the front of the tree in the foreground.
* The light shows up the texture of the tree very clearly here.
* The shadows are very dark (black in fact), and where the light fully hits the ground it is very cold and bright looking.
* The light works well in showing us the depth and structure of the objects in view.
* I like the way light is working in this photograph.

SEEING

Lighting designers need to be able to see the world around them with a clear understanding of the nature of light – in simple terms, if you look at any real-life situation you should be able to see and describe where the light source is and how it is affecting what is being lit (*see* Exercise 1, page 13). With a good understanding of how light works in a variety of situations we have a set of references to work from.

We must also have an understanding of the experiences we would expect our audience to be familiar with and have in common with us. After all, it is the audience who will ultimately be judging the effectiveness of our work. It is they that our work aims to influence.

It is most important to trust our own opinions on what we are looking at. There are no right or wrong answers – we simply need to find our own unique words or means to describe any given real-life scene. From this individuality of expression we derive our own artistic creativity.

EXERCISE 2
THE SOURCE OF LIGHT

Part 1

a. Look through a magazine or book for a colour photograph that shows a scene (typically a landscape – a holiday brochure would do well), or use a photograph of your own. The photograph should have an obvious strong light source, although the light source itself may not be in view. You may also choose to use the photograph on the following page as an example (*see* Fig. 4).

b. Describe to yourself how the light is affecting the objects in the picture in general terms – 'it is warm', 'it comes across the picture from the left', 'it is sunny and very bright'.

c. Does the light in the picture work effectively to make the photo a good one?

WHAT IS LIGHTING DESIGN?

Fig. 4 Reference for Exercise 2.

d. Specifically answer the following questions:

1. What colour is the light? Describe it.
2. Could you draw an arrow from outside or inside the picture indicating the light source?
3. What in the photo is made clearly visible by the light?
4. Which parts of the picture are in part shadow, which in full shadow?
5. Does the light create any particularly interesting effect on any part of the scene?
6. What, if anything, does the light lead your eye to?

If it helps, write down your impressions.

Part 2

You should also be able to answer these questions from Exercise 1:

* How many light sources are there?
* What part of the object is most brightly lit?
* Where do the shadows fall?

* Does the light on any object help it to blend in or stand out from the things around it?
* Do you like the way the light looks? Why?
* Could you move the photographer's viewpoint and feel the light would be more effective?

Repeat this exercise on a number of different photographs, striving to find contrasting scenes to analyse.

Analysis – Exercise 2

In this exercise you are adding to your visual vocabulary and general understanding of the light around you. The pictures you have chosen are by necessity framed and therefore not a total picture of any given scene; not all the information you might like to answer the questions is in view. Also, as you did not take the picture you cannot know the truth about what the light was really like when the picture was taken. So you must use your imagination about what you are seeing and how' it is arranged – much as you will expect an audience to look at a stage picture. Most importantly you are using your knowledge of the world around you to make a judgement about how the picture is lit. This is not really very different from the way you will need to address the needs of a dramatic piece. A lighting designer must react to similar stimuli and decide how the scene observed in rehearsal is to be lit on stage.

SEEING MORE

Lighting designers carry with them a range of 'real-life' references in their heads. They have looked at and understood the way in which light works to illuminate different situations. This looking at 'real light' never stops, it becomes a habit and a continual source of new ideas. This is not something that is difficult to develop – we all share an understanding of the colour, texture, illuminance, direction, and shadow-play of real light but perhaps cannot describe it as readily or effectively. It simply requires that the person has had the desire to look and describe for themselves rather than just take things for granted. It is not good enough to know that you like the way sunshine catches a person. You must also be able to quantify where the light sources are, where not, what colour they have, where they are coming from, how much light there is, and so on. All of this is simply a matter of seeing what is happening in front of you – we have to become expert 'see-ers'.

EXERCISE 3
LIGHT ON PEOPLE

This exercise is much the same as the previous one only looking at people rather than landscapes – in theatre terms; the actor, not the set:

a. Look through a magazine or book for a photograph (preferably in colour)

Fig. 5 Reference for Exercise 3.

that shows a person in close-up, *see* the example printed here. Again it will help you if an obvious strong light source is apparent.

You may also choose to start by using the photographs (Figs 5 & 6) as examples, or the one of Lord Attenborough on page 7.

b. Answer the following questions:

1. What colour is the light? Describe it.
2. Could you draw an arrow from outside the picture indicating the light source(s)?

Fig. 6 Reference for Exercise 3.

3. Is there more than one light source? Indicate the brightest.
4. What parts of the face are in shadow?
5. Does the light create any particularly interesting effect?
6. Is the background to the face important – is it lit lighter or darker? Does the light in the background help the figure to blend in or stand out from the things around it?
7. Do you like the way the light looks on the person? Why?

Repeat this exercise on a number of different photographs and even when you watch close-ups on TV or film. In fact try it on the next newsreader you see.

Analysis – Exercise 3

In a good photograph the lighting promotes or pushes the person towards us – the two-dimensional, flat image is given depth by the lighting and the figure is thus seen as more three-dimensional. With colour in the light and from the background we are given appropriate messages – soft focus or striking images depending on what is being 'sold' to us. This is how we are going to proceed as lighting designers – using such tools to sell a dramatic message to the audience. In this exercise we deviated from looking at real light in a real-world setting – getting our first taste of the power we are to wield on the stage.

SUMMARY

As lighting designers we need to develop a profound appreciation of real and artificial light sources. From this understanding of the world around us, gained by taking the time to look carefully, we can then digress. In digressing we can create lighting that is less than real but perhaps truer to the dramatic moment.

If we have some understanding of what each variation from the 'norm' means then we have a method for predicting how our audience will be affected by the lighting we provide for a scene. For example, if we understand what colour real sunlight is in a given situation, we could choose deliberately to enrich the colour on stage in order to heighten a particularly sunny scene, or make it colder to suit the context of a tragic scenario.

It is important to note that if we only ever try to reproduce 'real-life' light on stage even in supposedly real-life settings then the theatre world would be very boring indeed. This is not the point of analysing real light – after all, none of us really knew what the light was like on the deck of the *Bounty*, or on the planet 'Vulcan', or on Prospero's island. In our work as lighting designers, we cannot restrict ourselves to only creating the familiar. But we need a starting point, a marker, to work from – and this is the light of the real world.

2

THE EQUIPMENT WE USE

'Give Me the Tools'

THE LUMINAIRE

The equipment used to create most stage lighting is very simple. Let us start with the basic light-producing instrument which is often referred to as a lantern, but is more properly called a 'luminaire'.

Fig. 7 A luminaire.

LUMINAIRE

The term luminaire has become accepted as an international standard. Lantern, lamp, and light have better uses elsewhere (*see also* Spotlight box, page 23). The term unit is also acceptable in certain contexts.

If you have access to some equipment then by far the best way to understand it is by using it. The following exercises are designed to help you make sense of the various types of luminaire, their features and uses. If you do not have equipment readily available then the summaries of findings on pages 47–8 should help clarify what you may expect to find when you do get the chance. Read through the exercises anyway, or leave this chapter until you are able to get your hands on some luminaires.

EXERCISE 4
WHAT IS A LUMINAIRE?

Part 1
Taking any single luminaire at your

SAFETY NOTE

At this stage there is no need to connect your luminaire to a power supply.

disposal, identify the following external features:

a. The means to hang and secure the luminaire.
b. The locking devices (allowing both pan and tilt).

PAN AND TILT

Horizontal movement = pan
(*think of panorama*).

Vertical movement = tilt
(*think of tilting over*).

c. The aperture that lets out the light.
d. The device for holding a colour frame or gel in front of the aperture.

COLOUR HOLDERS

The colour filter is fitted into a frame that keeps it in shape as it becomes hotter. This frame slots into runners in front of the luminaire. In some cases the units have built-in gel frames. These are combined with clips and other safety devices to prevent the frame from falling out.

e. The means to get to and change the bulb within the luminaire.

It may be of use to sketch and label a basic diagram of your luminaire.

BULBS

The modern theatre bulb is made to heat up to very high temperatures and in doing so it becomes very fragile.

Quartz halogen or tungsten halogen bulbs must not be handled directly.

The outside of the bulb is very susceptible to uneven heating if grease or dirt is left on part of it.

Always follow the manufacturer's instructions when changing the bulb.

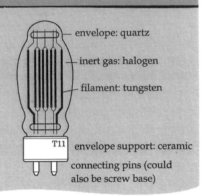

envelope: quartz

inert gas: halogen

filament: tungsten

T11 envelope support: ceramic

connecting pins (could also be screw base)

Fig. 8

BULB CHANGING

Always disconnect the luminaire from the power supply before opening the unit.

Part 2

Every luminaire has a method of allowing you to change the bulb (*see* safety box above) and with most this should let you have a glimpse of the interior – so now take the luminaire, find the way in and identify the following internal features:

a. The light source (or bulb).
b. The bulb holder.
c. The reflector behind the light source.
d. The pathway the light takes from bulb to stage.

AXIAL BULBS

In most luminaires the bulb is mounted vertically in front of the reflector which wastes some of the output of the lamp. Axial units have the bulb pointing down the body of the luminaire and so the reflector is able to send more light through the unit.

standard relationship between bulb and reflector

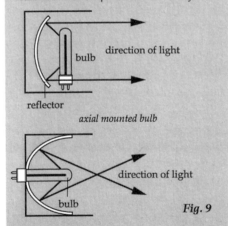

direction of light

bulb

reflector

axial mounted bulb

direction of light

bulb

Fig. 9

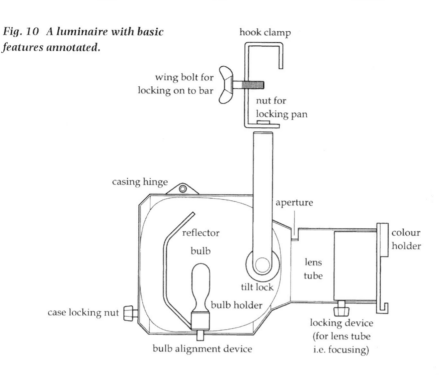

Fig. 10 A luminaire with basic features annotated.

hook clamp

wing bolt for locking on to bar

nut for locking pan

casing hinge

aperture

reflector

bulb

colour holder

lens tube

tilt lock

bulb holder

case locking nut

locking device (for lens tube i.e. focusing)

bulb alignment device

If you are new to the equipment you may have to ask for help or refer to the manufacturer's instructions at this point, but do not be put off.

few more features that need to be investigated. The next sections should help clarify this.

Analysis – Exercise 4

This exercise has helped define the basic elements of a luminaire and Fig. 10 should agree with your findings. The basic luminaire is a simple device holding a light-producing source which can be positioned and orientated to direct the light. In practice luminaires are a little more complicated than this and you will probably already realize that the real luminaire you are using has a

SPOTLIGHT

The term spotlight generally refers to any luminaire with a lens system.

It does not mean (as is often thought) a lantern that produces a hard-edged beam of light.

(*See also* Follow Spot box, page 41.)

A GUIDE TO LENS TYPES

There are a few distinct types of luminaire which have varied uses. They are clearly identifiable by whether or not they have a lens and what type of lens they use.

Lens Types	Luminaire Types
Profile lens	= profile spot
Fresnel lens	= fresnel spot
Pebble convex lens	= P.C. spot
Sealed beam unit	= par

Note: A unit with no lens but two reflectors = beam light (*see* Fig. 12).

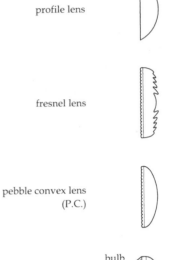

profile lens

fresnel lens

pebble convex lens (P.C.)

bulb

sealed beam unit (Par)

lens

reflector

Fig. 11 Lens types (above).

Fig. 12 Beam light: an unusual unit. No lens but reflector 2 makes sure all the light is reflected from the rear reflector. This parabolic reflector keeps the beam very narrow. The lower two diagrams show two different types of reflector.

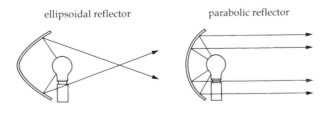

bulb

no lens

reflector 2

reflector 1

ellipsoidal reflector

parabolic reflector

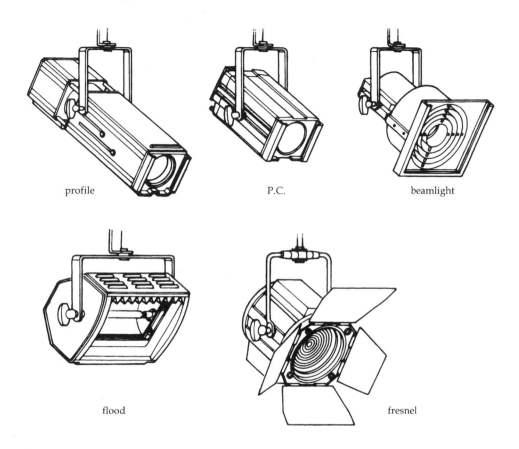

profile

P.C.

beamlight

flood

fresnel

Fig. 13 A range of equipment types.

EXERCISE 5
TYPES OF LUMINAIRE

a. Using the information provided above you should be able to clearly identify what type of luminaire you have been using in these exercises.

b. If you have access to more than one luminaire, identify all the other types in your stock and place them together in groups (floods, profiles, fresnels, and so on).

c. It is also probable that you will have luminaires manufactured by different companies, so also go through and identify the units by manufacturer.

d. Manufacturers will usually produce luminaires in a range of sizes, so now look for this information on each unit. Find out, for example, what wattage bulb the unit takes.

LUMINAIRE MANUFACTURERS

Include: Strand Lighting, CCT Lighting, ADB, ETC, Thomas, Selecon, Altman, Robert Juliat.

e. Profiles in particular are made to produce light from different distances to cover differing amounts of the stage – to do this they have various 'beam angles' (*see* Fig. 14 and box). See if any of your profiles have this identified by the manufacturer.

Analysis – Exercise 5

If you are lucky enough to be using some newer equipment you will find that the manufacturers obligingly label the unit with all the information you need concerning the name, manufacturer, and beam angle – in many cases the beam angle is actually part of the name.

Older units are less likely to include such information, but not to worry. Even if nobody knows what the units are called and therefore looking up how they may perform is impossible, the actual way they perform is best deduced by using them, so keep going and do not write-off the older equipment yet!

BEAM ANGLE

The beam angle is the diameter across the beam of light as it leaves the luminaire. All luminaires have a specific beam angle. A unit with two independently moving lenses has a range of beam angles, is usually a profile spot, and thus can be described as a zoom profile. (*See* Focus section, pages 47 & 93.)

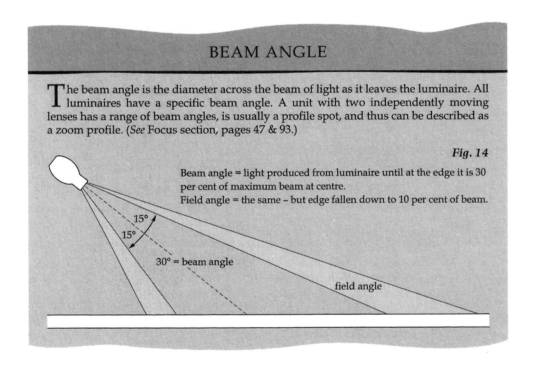

Fig. 14

Beam angle = light produced from luminaire until at the edge it is 30 per cent of maximum beam at centre.
Field angle = the same – but edge fallen down to 10 per cent of beam.

15°
15°
30° = beam angle
field angle

Fig. 15 A typical unit: a Strand zoom profile, the BRIO 25/50 (see also the CCT minuette profile, page 20).

NAMES OF OLDER EQUIPMENT

Manufacturers of older equipment used numbering to identify their products but they rarely refer to anything useful. In fact Strand's prolific early system referred to the design pattern of the unit. An example of this is the once ubiquitous and still widely used Patt 23 (Patt = Pattern).

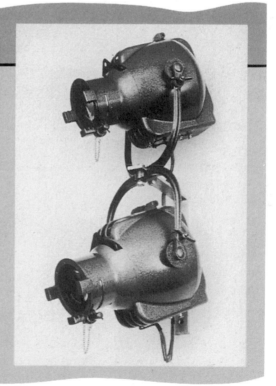

Fig. 16 Patt 23.

EXERCISE 6
KNOW YOUR EQUIPMENT

Create a blank chart using the headings in the example below and complete it for all the luminaires in your working space, possibly making separate charts for profiles, fresnels, and others. The example below shows a partly completed chart.

SYMBOLS

Symbols for the majority of luminaires are to be found on manufactured stencils or in CAD packages (*see* page 174). In some cases you may have to modify or use an alternative symbol. If you have access to a stencil, use it in the symbol column.

NAME	QTY	MAKE	SYMBOL	TYPE	POWER	NOTES
Source 4 26°		ETC		Profile	400 watts	Axial
Prelude 16/30		Strand		Profile	650 watts	Zoom
ADB F		ADB		Fresnel	1,000 watts	
Harmony PC		Strand		PC	1,000 watts	

N.B: *Indicates correct stencil symbol
> Indicates invented symbol

SUMMARY

Now we can identify the parts of a luminaire and the manner in which types of luminaire differ.

Seeing how basic the instruments are it is now important that we begin to use the equipment, gain confidence, and learn how the different types operate. The next chapter looks at how to rig and arrange luminaires safely within a performance space. If you are familiar with your theatre layout you may wish to move straight on to Chapter 4 which deals with using the luminaires.

3

THE THEATRE LAYOUT AND ELECTRICAL RESTRICTIONS

'Wherefore Art Thou?'

THE PERFORMANCE LAYOUT

To be safe and sure about what we are doing it is important to understand some basic technical aspects of the theatre layout. Every performance space – theatre, studio, church or school hall – is different, however most offer the basic layout shown in Fig. 17.

SOFT PATCH

Many lighting control boards will allow the circuit number to be changed as it relates to the socket in the theatre. This is particularly useful when touring a rig and taking the recorded lighting plot from venue to venue, as it means that a luminaire plotted as channel 1 can be designated the same number in another venue whatever the new venue's dimmer allocation – this is called soft patching.

PATCH SYSTEM

A patch system allows for the circuits of power controlled by individual dimmers to be allocated manually to whatever outlets are desired (*see* Fig. 125).

A fully operational and well-placed patch system allows for a limited power supply to be diverted to different luminaires even as a performance progresses.

FUSES

As a device to protect the user against surges in current or shorts the fuse has now been generally superseded by faster reacting and safer devices (such as the RCD or residual current device) which trip-out rather than blow when a problem occurs.

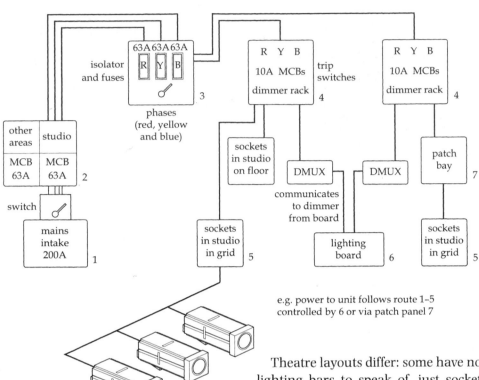

Fig. 17 A Studio-theatre layout.

1. Three-phase power in at 200 amps 220 volts.
2. Micro-circuit breaker (MCB) protects areas –
   one of which is the theatre supply at 63 amps.
3. A fuse for each phase (red, yellow, blue) and a
   main switch/isolator.
4. Dimmers in 'racks' each having their own MCB
   at 10 amps. The power is supplied via the
   dimmer to the socket outlets.
5. The lighting board operates as a remote control
   of the dimmers and usually communicates
   through a DMUX (de-multiplexing unit).
6. A patching bay is also shown allowing for
   greater routing of power from the second
   dimmer rack.

Theatre layouts differ: some have no lighting bars to speak of, just socket outlets; some have all the outlets in one large outlet bay, a 'patch bay'; whilst others have only a limited number of circuits that are therefore duplicated for ease of use.

EXERCISE 7
RESEARCHING THE SPACE

a. Allocate the elements in the diagram above into your working space.
b. Make a quick, rough sketch of your theatre layout.
c. Make a particular point of marking all the rigging positions (*see* Rigging Positions box opposite).

RIGGING POSITIONS

Luminaires may be hung from horizontal bars, rigged on vertical bars (booms) using boom arms, or placed on lighting stands of various adjustable heights. Some units will rest safely on the floor. Units may also be attached to the set as long as safety rules are adhered to.

A fixed network of horizontal bars is referred to as a grid.

A single short-flown horizontal bar is called a trapeze.

A group of joined horizontal bars is called a ladder (*see* Fig. 18).

(*See also* safety notes on Rigging Procedures, page 34.)

SAFETY CHAINS

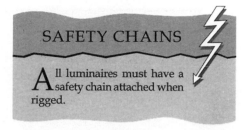

All luminaires must have a safety chain attached when rigged.

CABLING

Cable should be secured as appropriate, using tape or cable ties. Make sure no cables can cause trip hazards or be caught by scenery.

Fig. 18 Lighting positions (safety chains not shown).

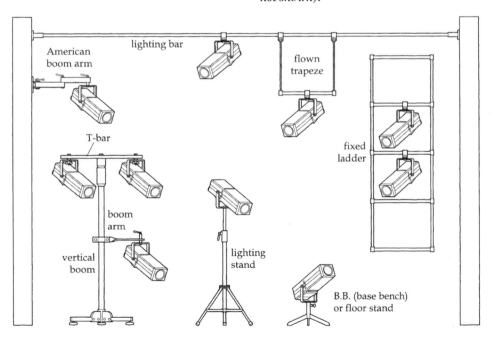

d. Note any safety requirements, particularly regarding rigging. Find out, for example, where lighting stands may be placed, or under what circumstances luminaires may be placed at floor level.

Analysis – Exercise 7

If no accurate plan of the lighting layout already exists it may be of great future use for you and others to turn your rough sketch into an accurate scale diagram. Most theatre spaces have accurate scale drawings for the

SOCKET OUTLETS

Most theatre spaces use a different plug and socket system to that in standard domestic use. The theatre system uses unfused plugs and sockets – the fuse device is allocated at the dimmer which makes it easier to replace.

The UK standard is the round-pin 15 amp plug/socket. The stronger, more securable Cee-Form type is also gaining in popularity.

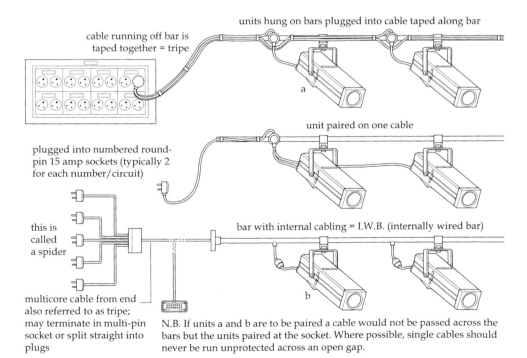

units hung on bars plugged into cable taped along bar

cable running off bar is taped together = tripe

a

unit paired on one cable

plugged into numbered round-pin 15 amp sockets (typically 2 for each number/circuit)

this is called a spider

bar with internal cabling = I.W.B. (internally wired bar)

b

multicore cable from end also referred to as tripe; may terminate in multi-pin socket or split straight into plugs

N.B. If units a and b are to be paired a cable would not be passed across the bars but the units paired at the socket. Where possible, single cables should never be run unprotected across an open gap.

Fig. 19 Diagram of plugs/sockets and cabling runs as described (including tripeing).

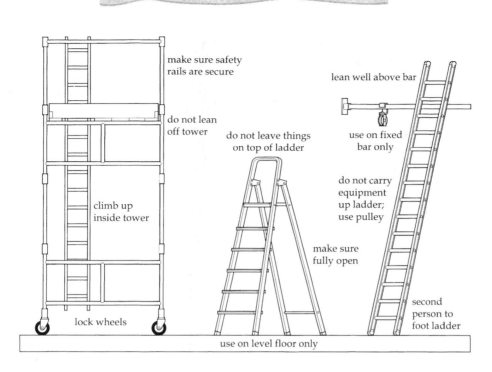

make sure safety
rails are secure

lean well above bar

do not lean
off tower

do not leave things
on top of ladder

use on fixed
bar only

do not carry
equipment
up ladder;
use pulley

climb up
inside tower

make sure
fully open

second
person to
foot ladder

lock wheels

use on level floor only

Fig. 20 Ladders and their usage.

use of designers but you may still find that you can usefully add to them. Certainly an accurate scale drawing showing rigging positions will be of great use when you move on to drawing lighting designs (*see* page 174) and for future use of the space generally.

(*see* page 174)

PAIRING

Units can be ganged together on to the same dimmer circuit with devices called splitters and grelcos.

Pairing of units occurs when there are not enough circuits available. The designer will lose individual control of the units.

POWER LIMITATIONS – OHM'S LAW

One aspect that must be considered in using the space is the type of power supply and its limitations. Only so many luminaires can be plugged into any particular socket, and where the power is limited only a certain number of sockets can be used simultaneously, which will restrict the number of circuits switched on at any one moment.

THE RIGGING PROCESS

It is important to rig quickly, efficiently and safely (*see* adjoining safety box). The following tips will help:

1. Make sure you understand the plan and know where everything has to go.
2. Label plug tops with removable white tape and marker pen so that in a mess of cable each can be easily identified.
3. Organize the work so that you move the ladder, or similar equipment, as little as possible – thus taking less time.
4. Work along lighting bars towards the plugging point, gathering and joining together (tripeing) cables as you go.
5. Check equipment is not faulty before you spend time putting it into the rig.
6. Point the unit roughly in the right direction to speed up focusing later.
7. Lock the unit off so that it will not move by accident, but not so tightly that it cannot be easily moved when focusing.

To work out how many luminaires you can use you need to know:

a. Their power rating (wattage).
b. The supply voltage (UK voltage is 230 volts).
c. The current capacity (number of amps) of the circuit you are using or fuse rating.

RIGGING DEVICES

When rigging at height always use equipment properly and safely (*see* Figs 19 & 20) and follow the manufacturer's instructions.

Wear a hard hat when people are working above you.

Always have someone footing the ladder.

Do not over-extend extendable ladders, climb too high, or lean out from them.

Lift equipment by rope, do not climb ladders with equipment.

Always use out-riggers where provided.

With specialist equipment such as tallescopes, always read safety instructions carefully before use.

Applying Ohm's Law (*see* box below) allows you to work out what power

OHM'S LAW

$$V = IR$$
(V = voltage, I = current, R = resistance)

Also

$$P = VI$$
(P = power)

Useful ways to remember them; PVC, VCR.

Note: UK mains supply in AC (alternating current) at 230 volts.

consumption the system will tolerate safely, and thus how many units you can plug in or fade-up at once.

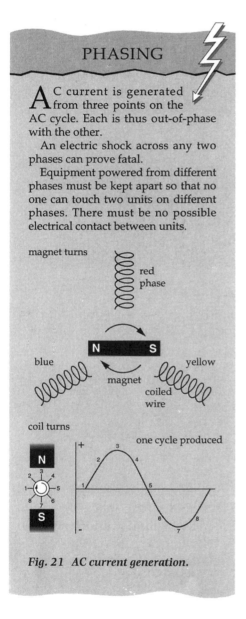

PHASING

AC current is generated from three points on the AC cycle. Each is thus out-of-phase with the other.

An electric shock across any two phases can prove fatal.

Equipment powered from different phases must be kept apart so that no one can touch two units on different phases. There must be no possible electrical contact between units.

magnet turns

red phase

N   S

blue

magnet

yellow

coiled wire

coil turns

+

one cycle produced

N

S

Fig. 21 AC current generation.

EXERCISE 8
OHM'S LAW – How Much Is too Much?

Part One
Find out what phase or phases the power that is supplied to your theatre space is connected to. Add this information to your sketch from the exercise above.

Part Two
To check you are being safe carry out the following calculations for your own theatre space:

a. The number of units you can plug into one of your sockets. Where you have outlets of various denominations (5 amp, 10 amp, 20 amp), do the calculation for one of each.
b. How big a rig can you put into your space? Calculate how much power your main fuse can take at any one time and/or any intermediary fuses, such as phase fuses.
c. It is also worth making a mental note of how much you can draw from a single standard 13 amp supply, so carry out this calculation also.

Analysis – Exercise 8
Answers:

a. For 230 volt and a 5 amp circuit – Use P = VI or P = 230 × 5 thus the circuit will tolerate 1,150 watts. For 230 volt and a 10 amp circuit – Use P = VI or P = 230 × 10 thus the circuit will tolerate 2,300 watts. For 230 volt and a 20 amp circuit – Use P = VI or P = 230 × 20 thus the circuit will tolerate 4,600 watts.

b. Typical answer for a 60 amp supply – Use P = VI or P = 230 × 60 thus the circuit will tolerate 13,800 watts.

c. For 230 volt and a 13 amp circuit – Use P = VI or P = 230 × 13 thus the circuit will tolerate 2,990 watts.

In practice a fuse rated 5 amp is generally considered a 1,000 watt or 1 kilowatt channel, 10 amp a 2 kilowatt channel.

EXERCISE 9
ELECTRICAL SAFETY

How good is your understanding of electrical safety? Answer the following questions:

1. What dictates the extent of an electric shock, the current or the voltage?

TREATMENT FOR ELECTRIC SHOCK

1. *Do not* put yourself in danger.
2. Turn off the power.
3. If you cannot turn off the power, push or drag the victim away from the source if they are not touching it, but do not put yourself in danger.
4. Apply first aid as necessary.
5. Call for help.

2. How much current is dangerous?
3. What factors affect the way we respond to an electrical shock?

Analysis – Exercise 9

The fatal factors concerned are the size of the current and what the current passes through. Very little current is required to cause a major shock if it passes across vital organs.

1–2mA	= Perceivable harmless shock.
5mA	= Unpleasant sensation, muscle spasm.
5–10mA	= Throw-off level, painful.
10–15mA	= Muscular contraction.
20–30mA	= Impaired breathing.
50mA	= Paralyse chest muscles.
100mA	= Ventricular fibrillation and death.

Note: Only 5 amps are used in the USA for the electric chair.

SUMMARY

Remember before attempting any rigging to make sure you are going to be safe in your use of both electrical and non-electrical equipment and that you understand the electrical limitations and general layout of the space itself. Safety should always be the number one concern. If in any doubt seek advice.

4

THE EQUIPMENT IN
USE - FOCUSING

'What Light through Yonder Window Breaks?'

HOW THE LUMINAIRE TYPES DIFFER

Most luminaires allow you to focus or alter the appearance of the light they produce. ('Focusing' can also refer to the general act of focusing all the units.) It is in focusing the units that we see how luminaires differ from each other, and what the various types are used for (*see also* Focusing information box, page 93). The following exercises underline these distinctions and will help you gain familiarity with the equipment.

EXERCISE 10
FOCUSING LUMINAIRES 1

a. Choose any luminaire and make a note of its name and type.

b. Rig the unit so that you can focus it whilst standing comfortably on the ground (*see* Rigging Positions, page 31).

SAFETY NOTE

It is important that you operate safely within your theatre space. If in any doubt, consult someone who knows.

You may wish to check with the Theatre Layout chapter, especially concerning rigging and electrical circuiting of your space (*see* page 30).

c. Rig the unit at a workable distance from a blank wall. A good distance would be the same as the usual rigging height in your working space.

d. Connect the unit to a dimmable circuit or mains power and switch on.

e. Find and use the focusing device on the unit. Explore its full range by moving the focus from one extreme to another, then answer the following questions:

1. Does the lantern focus the light to give a hard or soft edge to the beam when it hits the stage?
2. Does the size alter much in focusing?
3. Is anything such as a shutter or barn-door used to shape the beam?
4. What other devices does the luminaire have and how do they affect the beam? (*See* box right.)

SAFETY NOTE

Luminaires get very hot. Always handle with care and make sure you know which parts of the unit to handle. Protective gloves are recommended.

BULB ALIGNMENT

Luminaires often have external methods of aligning the bulb. Often the bulb alignment will also allow the beam to be deliberately flat (uniform across the beam) or peaked (brighter in the middle) as is useful with gobos.

Note: Adjust the alignment carefully as over-enthusiastic movements can cause the bulb to fail.

Repeat for as many luminaires as you wish.

Fig. 22 Note the focus knobs on the side of this unit.

LUMINAIRE	SIZE VARIATION	LOOK (HARD/SOFT)	BEAM SHAPE DEVICE	DEVICES	NOTES
Minuette fresnel	Very good	Soft	Barn-door	None	
Minuette profile	Good	Both	Shutters	Gobo, iris (see Fig. 26)	Zoom, condenser lens
Patt 750	Poor	Soft	Top hat	None	Beam light
Source 4	Poor	Both	Shutters	Gobo, iris	Very bright

Note: Exercises 11 and 12 investigate luminaires further, you may wish to look at these exercises whilst you are still in your working space.

You may like to keep the information for future reference – perhaps by filling in a chart in the same way as in the example above.

Fig. 23 Top hat (top left), barn-door (top right) and shutters (bottom).

Analysis – Exercise 10

From your experimentation you should now be learning how your equipment functions. In particular you should have found that the luminaire types behave in specific ways. These are summarized in the chart below (check against your own findings):

LUMINAIRE TYPE	SIZE VARIATION	LOOK (HARD/SOFT)	BEAM SHAPE	SPECIAL TYPES	NOTES
flood 	none	soft	barn-door	cyc' flood	
fresnel 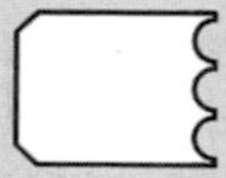	very good	soft	barn-door	none	
PC 	very good	soft	barn-door	none	
profile 	poor	hard and soft	shutters, iris, gobo, mask	follow spot, axial bulb, zoom	
zoom profile 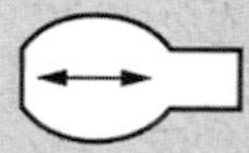	very good	hard and soft	shutters, iris, gobo, mask	follow spot, axial bulb, discharge unit	
parcan 	none	soft	barn-door or top hat	low voltage	
beam light 	poor	soft	barn-door	follow spot, low voltage	

To put your knowledge of equipment into perspective carry out the next exercise which should clarify what the equipment is best used for.

EXERCISE 11
LUMINAIRE TYPES – Quiz

From your knowledge of the luminaires that you have been using and from the chart above answer the following questions:

1. Which luminaire type has the potential to cover the most area?
2. Which luminaire type gives the most precise control over the shape of the beam?
3. Which luminaire type gives the brightest/punchiest light output for its wattage?
4. Which luminaire types have no focusing capability?

CONDENSER LENS

Some luminaires have an extra non-movable lens directly in front of the bulb. The condenser lens has the effect of collecting the light output from the bulb and directing it into the lens system in front. Units with a condenser lens will be brighter per watt than those without.

THE FOLLOW SPOT

This is the term for a luminaire rigged so that it can be hand-operated during a performance, typically to 'follow' an actor. It often has an integral iris, internal dimming (often mechanical), and semaphore mechanical colour changing.

The follow spot is most usually a zoom profile but can also be a discharge unit (*see* Discharge Units box, page 42).

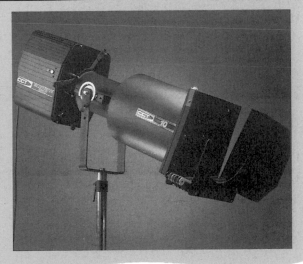

Fig. 24 Typical follow spot.

DISCHARGE UNITS

This is the term for luminaires that use a light source different from the tungsten halogen bulb. The source of light is created by a spark of electricity jumping between two electrical poles which makes for a very bright light and one of a different colour temperature to the tungsten units (*see* page 83).

The units use transformers to create the high current needed to jump between the poles. As such they can only be dimmed with mechanical dimming shutters.

Discharge units are often follow spots, or large fresnels. They are often named after their source. Popular examples include CSI (Compact Source Iodide), CID and HMI units.

5. Which luminaire types allow for focusable but large area cover?
6. Which luminaire type allows for hard focus at different sizes of beam?
7. Which two luminaire types are most alike?

Analysis – Exercise 11
Answers:

1. The flood.
2. The profile.
3. The parcan.
4. The flood.
5. The fresnel or PC.
6. The zoom profile.

7. The fresnel and PC, or parcan and beam light.

All luminaires allow for a colour to be slotted in front of the unit. Most also allow for some shaping of the beam – with a shutter, barn-door or top hat. The profile also allows for quite precise focusing and so additional devices may be used, for example, the gobo, a pierced metal stencil (*see* Fig. 26).

EXERCISE 12
FOCUSING LUMINAIRES 2

Rig your equipment so that you can focus whilst standing on the ground. You may wish to rig more than one unit at a time so that you can make comparisons between them. To further your knowledge of the equipment, investigate your luminaires in order to answer the following questions:

1. When you focus a fresnel or PC what are you moving?
2. Is the fresnel bigger or smaller when the focus is pulled towards the back of the luminaire?
3. When you focus a profile what are you moving?
4. When you focus a zoom profile when is the beam the smallest – with the lenses far apart or close together?
5. Which shutter on a profile affects the bottom of the light beam?

6. Which door of the barn-door on a fresnel or PC affects the top of the light beam?

7. Explain why the answers to 5 and 6 are different.

8. What shape is the beam of light leaving a parcan? How is this different to the other equipment, for example, a fresnel?

Analysis – Exercise 12

The following answers apply to all models of any specific luminaire type:

1. The bulb holding unit (often called the bulb tray) and reflector.

2. Smaller.

3. The lens.

4. Furthest apart.

5. The shutter on the top of the unit.

6. The top barn-door.

7. In a profile the shutter affects the beam of light before it goes through the focal point and thus the image of the shutter crosses over to the other side of the beam. The same is true of the side shutters – the left shutter affects the right side of the beam. In a fresnel the barn-door affects the beam after it has passed through the focal point of the beam, so the left door affects the left side of the beam.

8. The nature of a par lamp causes the beam from a parcan to be oval, rather than circular (Fig. 29) as is the case with all other units (*see* Par box overleaf).

EXERCISE 13
USING THE LUMINAIRE

The aim of this exercise is to develop further an understanding of focusing. Using the same set-up as in the previous exercise carry out the following:

a. Choose something within your working space to focus on. Rectangular or square shapes such as windows or doors are ideal to start with.

b. Rig a luminaire and attempt to light the object you have chosen with it. Try and shape the unit as precisely as you can to the object, using focus, and shutter or barn-door.

c. Repeat the exercise using a different object and perhaps a different luminaire type.

d. As you repeat the exercise make a point of trying to choose luminaires that will light the objects that you have chosen, in other words try to match the size of the unit with the expected size of the beam from your luminaire.

e. Repeat the exercise focusing on smaller and more difficult shapes.

Analysis – Exercise 13

There is really no substitute for using the equipment to gain familiarity. Learning the relative beam sizes of your equipment will prepare you for the sometimes difficult task of choosing equipment when formulating a

THE PAR

The par lamp can be described as a sealed beam unit (SBU). It contains a bulb (set axially), reflector and lens all in the one unit. It is the fixed nature of this arrangement that produces such an impressive amount of light.

Because of the oval shape of the beam the sealed beam unit within a parcan can rotate, allowing the lighting designer to orientate the oval to maximum advantage.

Unlike other luminaires the parcan itself cannot be focused - the bulb unit has to be changed in order to alter the beam angle.

Fig. 25 Parcan manufactured by Thomas.

lighting design. The more you use the equipment the easier this task will become.

The next exercise continues this process by adding more luminaire devices to your repertoire.

EXERCISE 14
USING THE GOBO, IRIS AND DOUGHNUT

Making use of the same set-up as in the previous exercises carry out the following:

a. Focus a profile on to a flat surface such as a wall.
b. Add a gobo or an iris to the profile and focus it hard (clearly) on to the wall.
c. Repeat the exercise with a new luminaire. Choose a gobo that you think will join up neatly with the first one, for example, set two window gobos side-by-side, or two iris luminaires to look like eyes.
d. Repeat the exercise as many times as you want until the wall is covered. If you cannot achieve what

you are aiming for at the first time of trying, choose another luminaire, or set yourself a different task with the same luminaire. Remember, a zoom profile will allow you more size options than non-zoom profile.

e. You may like to reproduce some of the shapes illustrated in Fig. 27.

f. If you are using gobos and are not getting a sharp enough image try using a doughnut (*see* Fig. 28). Figure 1 shows light split into beams by a simple gobo.

Analysis – Exercise 14

Once again the trick with this exercise is luminaire choice, and not setting yourself too hard a task! Focusing and luminaire choice are central to all lighting design.

SUMMARY

With a good knowledge of the following luminaire types you are well on the way to mastering the main technical aspects of the job.

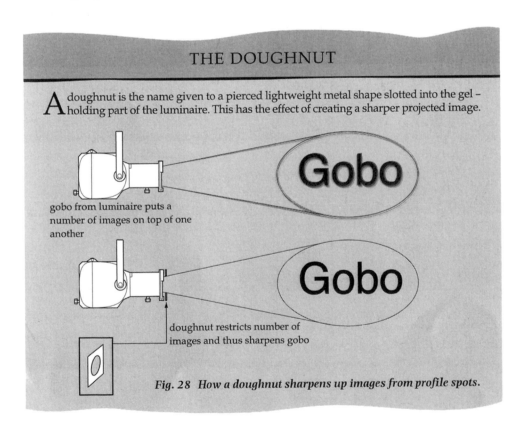

THE DOUGHNUT

A doughnut is the name given to a pierced lightweight metal shape slotted into the gel – holding part of the luminaire. This has the effect of creating a sharper projected image.

Gobo

gobo from luminaire puts a number of images on top of one another

Gobo

doughnut restricts number of images and thus sharpens gobo

Fig. 28 How a doughnut sharpens up images from profile spots.

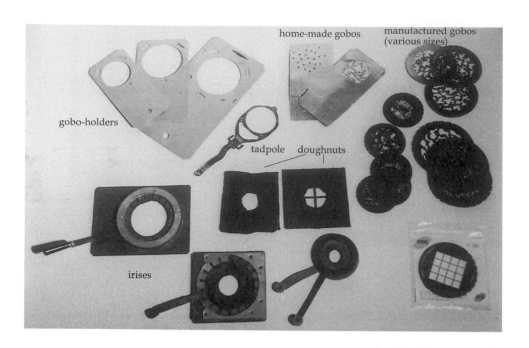

home-made gobos

manufactured gobos (various sizes)

gobo-holders

tadpole   doughnuts

irises

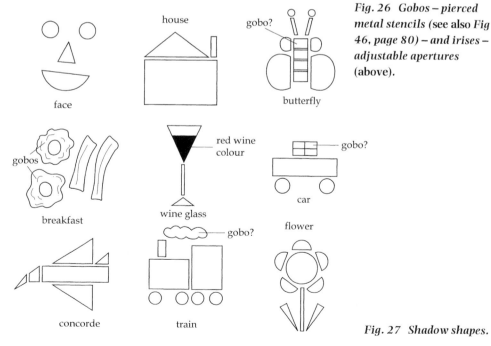

Fig. 26 Gobos – pierced metal stencils (see also Fig 46, page 80) – and irises – adjustable apertures (above).

house

gobo?

face

butterfly

gobos

breakfast

red wine colour

wine glass

gobo?

car

flower

concorde

gobo?

train

Fig. 27 Shadow shapes.

PROFILE SPOTS

Lanterns that can be focused to 'profile' an object. Examples include the gobo, iris, mask and shutter. Good beam projection. Various types, for example beam angles, wattage.

General Notes

Two independent lenses = zoom profile.
Two shutter systems = bi-focal spot.
Axial-mounted bulb = better light output.
Condenser lens = extra non-focusable lens, giving better light output.
Units may accept alternative lenses to adjust beam-angle range.

Usage

1. Good for precise shaping of beam when required and hard edges.
2. Used for gobos.
3. Optics give good beam projection useful for projecting light over distance.
4. Good for tight and precise specials.
5. Hard-edged beam has made it a favourite as a follow spot, that is, zoom and discharge versions.

FRESNEL SPOTS

Lanterns that can be focused over a wide range of beam angles, producing a soft beam. There are various types.

General Notes

Beam shape controlled with barn-door shutters only.

Usage

1. Good for large area cover.
2. Good for colour washes.
3. Good beam projector at medium or close distances (see General Cover, Exercise 43, page 108).
4. Good for soft-edged specials at close distance.

PC SPOT

Pebble convex – produces better light than a fresnel.

Usage

1. Generally same notes as for the fresnel only the PC is usually better at light reproduction and so better at distance.
2. Usually closes to smaller area than the fresnel and thus better for specials.

PARCAN

A sealed-beam unit – pars may be swapped in cans.

Note: Voltage may be 110 volts – series splitter needed.

Usage

1. As a powerful source of light – particularly with dark colours.
2. Narrow beam units good for soft, but potentially very bright, specials.

Note: See also The Birdy, above.

THE BIRDY

The birdy is the most popular way in which low-voltage units are used on stage. The birdy is like a very small version of the parcan – it is called a birdy because it is 'one under par'! The birdy uses a 12 volt bulb and thus needs to be connected to a transformer in order to be used on conventional dimmers. Like the par, a number of beam-angle bulbs are available for use. These vary from 11–60 degrees, and usually 50–75 watts.

Fig. 29   Standard black birdy (left), customized silver birdy (top right), and birdy bulb unit (N.B. dichroic reflector).

BEAM LIGHT

Has two reflectors, no lens, and produces a narrow beam like a searchlight.

Usage
As for the parcan. Its ability to alter size has made it popular as a soft follow spot.

FLOOD

A large beam angle, no lens = no focus.

Usage
1. Specialized version used to light cycloramas.
2. Size of beam makes it useful as a working light.

5

BEGINNING TO LIGHT THE PERFORMER

'X' marks the spot

In the last two chapters we became familiar with the luminaire and a basic theatre layout. Now that we are getting used to the equipment, let us return to our growing ideas of the way light works (*see* Chapter 1) and try some exercises to increase this understanding by at last manipulating the light source ourselves.

The exercises that follow may be carried out in any useable space. For the purposes of analysing and commenting on expected results I have used a space and rigging position as illustrated in Fig. 30.

EXERCISE 15
'X' MARKS THE SPOT

a. Place a chair in a central position in your performance space.
b. Take any suitable luminaire. Position and focus the unit so that it will light somebody sitting in the chair. You may place the luminaire anywhere in your working space.
c. Use the luminaire at full power – it can be connected to a mains supply rather than a dimmable source.
d. Take another luminaire and repeat 'b' making sure that there are 2–3

ADVICE ON CARRYING OUT THE EXERCISES

If you are unsure as to how to proceed with an exercise – what units to use and so on,

Either
Re-read the earlier sections on equipment

Or
Decide on a place to start, choose a unit and try it. If it works – good. If not try again. With the more creative exercises – if you do not want to start by sketching your ideas on paper first then use the same principle as above – try a unit, a colour, or an angle and build your finished result bit by bit.

Fig. 30

BASIC RIG: PLAN

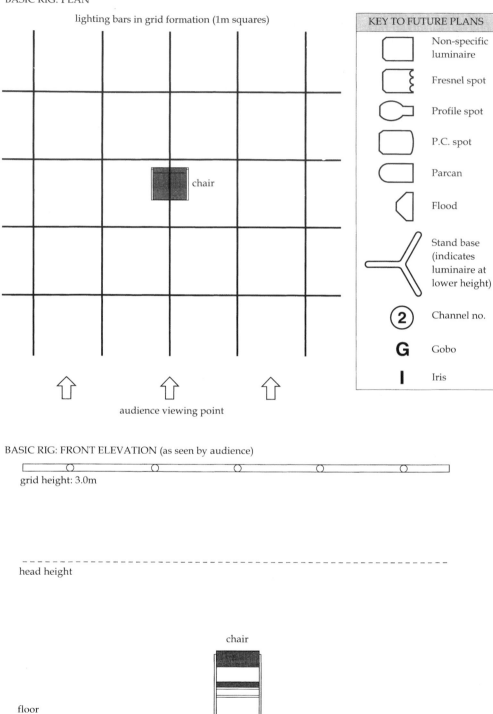

lighting bars in grid formation (1m squares)

chair

audience viewing point

KEY TO FUTURE PLANS

	Non-specific luminaire
	Fresnel spot
	Profile spot
	P.C. spot
	Parcan
	Flood
	Stand base (indicates luminaire at lower height)
2	Channel no.
G	Gobo
I	Iris

BASIC RIG: FRONT ELEVATION (as seen by audience)

grid height: 3.0m

head height

chair

floor

BASIC RIG: SIDE ELEVATION

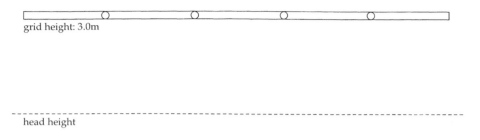

grid height: 3.0m

head height

chair

floor

audience
viewing point

BASIC RIG: 3D IMPRESSION

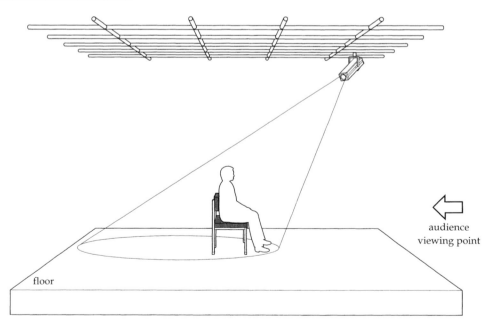

audience
viewing point

floor

FOCUSING TIPS

When focusing a luminaire remember that the light is needed on the object, not just the floor. Always think three-dimensionally.

If you are directing the event, stand outside the area and look at what the light is doing, or stand in the light with your back to it, using your shadow as a reference.

Do not look into the beam – it will damage your eyes, and, once dazzled, you will not be able to see clearly what you are doing.

(*See* page 93, for Focusing with a team.)

RIGGING LUMINAIRES

If you are unsure about the safe way to rig and use the equipment go back to Chapter 3 for help.

If you are in any doubt about the safety requirements of your theatre space seek help before continuing.

metres (or yards) at least between the two units. Use as many different lantern types as possible, so that you are also adding to your equipment knowledge.

e. Repeat, again making sure that no two units are less than 2–3 metres (or yards) apart. The exact distance will depend on your working space.

f. Keep adding units until you feel the chair is 'well surrounded'. Remember that you can place units above, below and behind the chair.

g. Get a volunteer to sit in the chair. If you are alone use the chair only or substitute it for some more solid, three-dimensional object.

h. Sit in front of, and at a reasonable distance from the chair, object or person. You now become the audience.

(It is also possible to do this exercise with yourself in the chair and a reasonably large mirror where you would otherwise have been sitting as the audience.)

i. In a general state of darkness turn on each unit individually and, looking at the effect it has on the person or object, answer the following questions:

1. How much of the subject is visible?
2. Would it be uncomfortable to watch an actor play a scene of some length in this light?
3. Does the light give any particular atmosphere to the subject? If so, what, and why?
4. Can you think of a particular use for this light source – either dramatic or scenic?
5. Does this light source remind you of anything you have seen elsewhere?
6. Was your choice of luminaire a good one?

DBO

A general state of darkness in a theatre setting is described as a black-out or dead black-out (DBO).

Analysis – Exercise 15

This exercise starts the process of identifying luminaire positions from the angle that they light the subject. From this we derive the six main terms: front light, back light, side light, cross light, top light, and up light. From these we then obtain less mainstream terms such as steep top, shallow cross, and three-quarter back light (*see* Fig. 31). It is important

that we begin to make some sense of these lighting angles. You may want to repeat Exercise 15 on several occasions, reviewing your thoughts as your skills develop.

Now that you have completed the exercise do you agree with the following conclusions?

1. Front light is better for seeing the subject.
2. Angles other than front ones are more dramatic.
3. The sharper the angle, the more dramatic the appearance of the subject (*see* Exercise 17 for more on side light).
4. Up light looks most unusual of all.

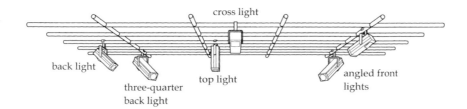

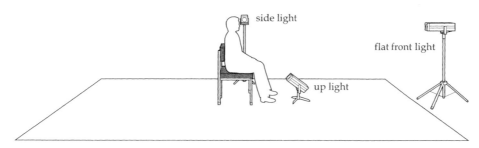

Fig. 31 Basic angles of light.

5. On its own, a scene would be difficult to sustain in back light only (*see* Exercise 20 for more on back light).

How much you agree or disagree with these statements is not important – you have to develop your own opinion about how light works. The important thing is that you are thinking in this way.

This exercise requires a choice of luminaire that focuses reasonably tightly on to the subject – your choice of equipment would have greatly enhanced or detracted from your result – how did you do? The process of choosing luminaires becomes an essential feature of every lighting design exercise from now on, and particularly so in the next few chapters.

EXERCISE 16
USING LUMINAIRES IN COMBINATION

For this exercise *either* save time by using the same rig as for the previous exercise – adding to it if necessary to fulfil all the requirements of the exercise *or* rig nine luminaires as illustrated in Fig. 32. The units will need to be connected to individual dimmable circuits

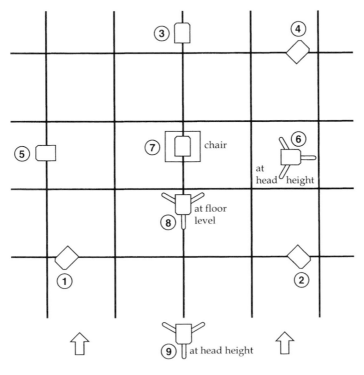

Fig. 32 Luminaires illustrated.

1. Front right.
2. Front left.
3. Back.
4. Three-quarter back.
5. Cross.
6. Side.
7. Top.
8. Up.
9. Flat front.

LIGHTING CONTROL

Stage lighting is controlled by lighting boards, either manual or memory. The former requires an operator to set dimmer levels by hand for each cue, the latter stores the levels for later playback. Both can have timers and various other helpful devices.

and thus a lighting control is required (*see* page 179).

Part 1

Using any *two* luminaires for each case, light the subject as described below:

a. Clearly
b. Mysteriously
c. Dramatically.

Also, try using two different types of luminaire on each occasion.

Part 2

Use any three luminaires to light the subject as described below:

a. Brightly
b. Eerily
c. Fiercely.

Analysis – Exercise 16

This exercise is about building your confidence in decision making. For the first time the level of light you are using from each unit comes into play and you must make creative decisions about what the descriptive terms mean. Once again there are no wrong answers, rather a continuing process of making judgements based on choice of lighting position and the amount of light. These exercises are particularly rewarding when carried out with a partner or within a group so that those around you can offer their opinions on the effectiveness of your vision.

LEVELS OF LIGHT

The first and most important lesson to learn about light levels is *not to use more than you need.* It is easy to believe that more is better when it comes to light. Just as we have a natural inclination to look towards the brightest object, so our eyes seems happiest when working the least. Our eyes often seem to be demanding more and more light when actually using less light creates subtlety of mood and generally greater visual interest. As with many artistic endeavours the key phrase here is *less is more.* To help develop an understanding of this it is useful to have in mind the concept that when selecting a luminaire to build a scene the initial aim should be to use it at no more than around 50 per cent. An important aspect of using varying amounts of light from several units is the contrast between units at different levels (*see* Exercise 19).

Theatre lighting designers generally rely on their eyes to make judgements concerning light levels, but it can be otherwise assessed.

Intensity of a light source is measured in candela. The amount of light falling on an object, known as illuminance, varies according to many factors – number of units used, wattage, distance from source to object, and so on. The unit of illuminance is the lumen. Lumens per square metre are called lux, lumens per square foot are called footcandles. The ratio of footcandles to lux is 1:10.76.

An ordinary photographic light meter can be used to measure illuminance by setting the film speed dial to ASA 100 and aiming the meter at a white card. Read the shutter speed required for an aperture setting of f/4 and interpret this as a whole number not a fraction – one sixtieth becomes sixty. This gives the approximate number of footcandles. Multiply by ten to convert to lux.

Fig. 33 Light creating texture on stage. A Midsummer-Night's Dream. *Contact Theatre Co.*

EXERCISE 17
TEXTURE

Texture is an important aspect of the lighting designer's world. This is a quick exercise using a front light and a side light (luminaires one and six from the previous exercise).

a. Find an object that you can bring into your working space that has a notable texture to it – a stage flat of a

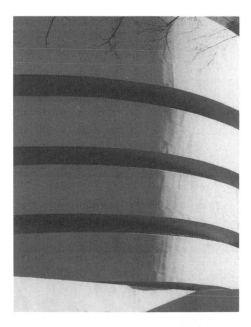

Figs. 34 Light glancing across objects to reveal texture and depth (compare also Figs 3–6, and Fig. 46).

rough plastered wall or brickwork, something with the texture of rough wood, even a loose flowing garment will suffice.

b. Focus your two lights onto it, the side light just skimming the surface.

c. Note the difference between the two.

Analysis – Exercise 17

You should find in this exercise that the front light presents you with very little of the texture of the object whereas the side light shows it up clearly, even exaggerating it. In the context of the exercise it is particularly important to note that given a rather flat-looking piece of scenery a very acute lighting angle will highlight even the most meagre of textures – the top light would have worked in a similar way. The two lighting angles we have used here are extremes but nevertheless make the point that the more acute the angle the more an object's dimensionality is displayed – this is true in all cases.

FLAT LIGHTING

A term often used (and misused) meaning that the light is causing few or no shadows on the object in view (usually the actor). Or, more likely, too many units are washing out all potential shadows. No highlighting, definition or three-dimensional effect comes from such flat light.

EXERCISE 18
BUILDING A PICTURE

Taking the same audience viewpoint, use as many luminaires from your rig as you think are necessary to create some lighting that you feel expresses how a well-lit subject should look. Take your time with this, choosing levels and looking at all the available units in turn and what they do, adding and subtracting units until you are happy with the result.

A STATE

The term for the lighting used at any particular time, or for a particular moment or scene in a performance is a lighting state.

With your lighting state before you, carry out the following:

a. Take out the luminaire that you feel makes the least contribution to the picture. Try as many as you like until you feel that you have chosen the right one.

b. Go on repeating 'a'. – each time taking out one more luminaire – until you are down to your last unit.

Analysis – Exercise 18

If you have used very few units to begin with then it will not take long to get down to a single unit. Also, by the time you do get down to one unit the lighting picture may well have altered drastically from what you started with. However the point of the exercise is to make you test and evaluate the decisions you made when building the picture in the first place.

Creating a state can take some time and it is usual for the lighting designer, with encouragement from the director and set designer, to take time over adding to and taking from the state before reaching a final look. It is important when going through this process to continue to evaluate the balance between the various luminaires and not to over-light and end up with redundant units.

This is an important exercise to help build the discernment required by a lighting designer; perhaps repeat it a number of times starting out with a different initial state on each occasion.

KEY LIGHT

A 'key light' is the lighting source that dominates a state – in other words the brightest apparent source of light. In a naturalistic setting this may represent sunlight, moonlight, a street light on a darkened night road, and so on. Even in an abstract state, where no real source need be suggested, the use of a key source is thought of as visually appealing.

EXERCISE 19
KEY LIGHT

This exercise uses the same rig and audience viewpoint as Exercise 16.

a. Choose any one of your luminaires and put it at 100 per cent – this is your key light source.
b. Add other luminaires to complement your key but so that the key remains dominant.
c. Repeat the exercise twice more starting with different units in your rig.
d. Before repeating the exercise for any other units read the exercise analysis below then repeat for all your remaining units in turn.

You may like to make a record of your analysis of the effectiveness of individual sources by filling in a chart (*see* example on page 60). My belief about the way in which the angles of light work is summarized in just such a chart at the end of this chapter.

LUMINAIRE OUTPUT VALUES (LEVELS)

Any exercise using luminaires at relative values assumes all units in the rig to be of the same light output – adjust for your rig as necessary.

SOURCE	CLARITY	DRAMA	ATMOSPHERE	SUN KEY?

Fig. 35 Actor light with key light source.

Analysis – Exercise 19

It may be that even in Exercise 16 you were drawn to creating a key source. General opinion is that using a key gives a more satisfactory look, as well as being more realistic. It is more realistic because in a real situation the light on any object is rarely even. A strong key source, such as bright sunlight, is particularly satisfactory to look at. Also, a more pleasing result will be achieved by using a key source that does not hit the actor directly from in front, behind or either side – the use of a seemingly less symmetrical angle will appear more realistic.

The main decision to make, after choosing a key source, is how to reinforce it from within the rest of the rig. A single key light source may suffice for a scene, especially if it sufficiently lights the face and makes the actor passably visible. But actors often need more than just one source of light to be clearly visible, or to give them greater substance on stage.

In such cases the decision is one of whether to use units that fall close in angle to the key light or more radically contrast with it (*see* Fig. 49). Both of these solutions are acceptable but create different finished products. The former helps support the key as a realistic source, the latter helps make more of the actor visible.

EXERCISE 20
BACK LIGHT

Once again the rig for Exercise 16 can be utilized, but actually we need only concern ourselves with luminaires one, two and three. The audience viewpoint remains the same.

a. Light the subject using the two front lights at 30 per cent, and the back light at full. The key should be the back light.
b. Look at your subject but also be aware of whatever is behind.
c. Without taking your eye off the subject snap out the back light – what do you see?
d. After a pause (allowing your eyes to adjust) reverse the exercise by snapping on the back light.
e. Read the exercise summary and then repeat the exercise if you feel that you need to.

SNAP

The act of turning on or off a luminaire or a lighting state with a zero time value is known as a snap.

Analysis – Exercise 20

Unlike most of the previous exercises this one presupposes a particular result. If you are having difficulty seeing the result then it may be because of some peculiarity of your circumstances – however, the exercise should be successful, if only to a limited extent.

What this exercise is trying to demonstrate is the role of light placed behind a person or object – back light. Back light is used to pull the subject away from the objects behind. You should find that with the back light dominating the picture the subject is pushed towards you and the background recedes. Without the back light the subject appears further away and less distinguishable from the background. Indeed in some cases without the back light the subject may actually blend in with the background in such a way that the distinction between the two is almost lost.

The role of back light to project the actor and therefore the drama towards the audience cannot be understated (*see* Fig. 36). It is a very powerful tool – especially when the distance between actor and audience is particularly large.

Fig. 36 Back light silhouettes the figure of Macbeth.

Fig. 37 Where back light is evident it separates the actors from the dark background. The History of Mr Polly. *Contact Theatre Co.*

In such a case the lighting designer needs all available resources to connect the two to make the drama work. In these circumstances, back light is the strongest of allies.

SUMMARY

This chapter has dealt with the manner in which different lighting angles enhance or detract from a stage picture. The value of back light and the use of acute angles to reveal texture should now have started to become apparent. How a lighting designer believes each angle works in isolation or as part of a state is a matter of personal preference and artistic choice.

The chart below outlines the nine basic angles seen in the exercises above and in Fig. 38. It discusses whether an angle is good for visual clarity or for dramatic atmosphere, what this atmosphere may be, and whether we would consider any particular lighting angle acceptable for the most basic of key sources – sunlight.

The nine lighting angles discussed here have been chosen because they

SOURCE	CLARITY	DRAMA	ATMOSPHERE	SUN KEY?
Front light from right	Yes, most useful	Not very dramatic	Neutral	Yes, but likely to lead to over-lighting
Front light from left	As above. The choice of left or right is a matter of personal preference			
Back light	No use on its own Adds real clarity	Most dramatic used with others	On its own it is very spooky	Yes, but a bit too centred on actor
¾ Back light	As back light above	As back light above	Shows more of the real actor but still a bit spooky	Yes, the off-centre angle is more realistic
Cross light	Of some use, generally poor visibility	Very effective	Very good to look at – shows texture well	Yes, as it originates from high angle
Side light	As above but less realistic	Very effective	Very good to look at – shows texture well	Only good for rising or setting sun perhaps?
Top light	No, too many odd shadows cast	Yes, very strong on the actor	Aggressive	Unlikely source, (except equator midday sun?)
Up light	No, too many really odd shadows cast	Yes, but too odd to be used often	Very spooky	No
Flat light	Yes	No – too much made visible	For third degree inquiry?	No

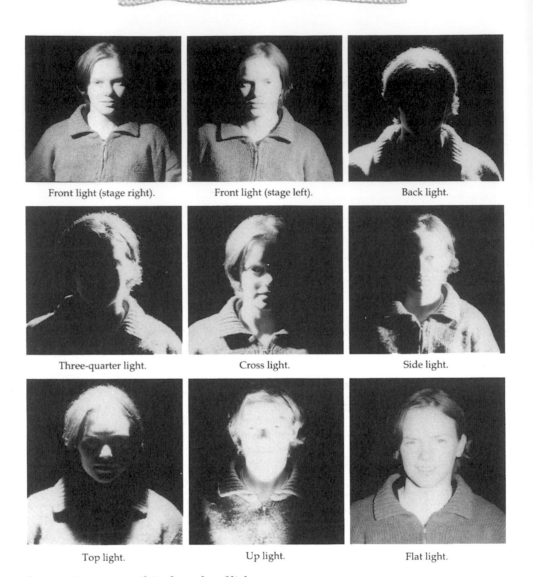

Front light (stage right). | Front light (stage left). | Back light.

Three-quarter light. | Cross light. | Side light.

Top light. | Up light. | Flat light.

Fig. 38 Comparison of single angles of light on an actor.

represent the extremes of each concept. Between them are 360 degrees of alternatives – and in more than one plane – and each with its own particular variation on what we have already seen. The next chapters deal with using these angles to create stage lighting, starting with the use of colour.

6

COLOUR AND LIGHT

'It's not Easy Being Green'

COLOUR

Colour is perhaps the most emotive of all the elements concerned with stage lighting, and it also brings to our attention a few questions about light itself. In much the same way as we have already examined our perceptions about the nature of real light, we will start using colour in our lighting by examining what we already feel about colour generally.

All luminaires allow for the fixing of a filter in front to affect the colour of the light produced. The need to create mood with colour has also led to some

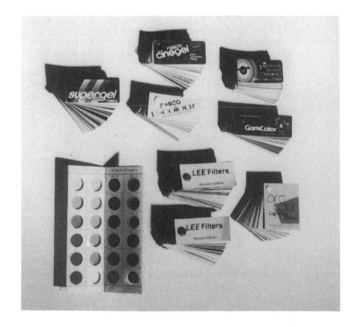

Fig. 39 Manufacturers' colour sample books (swatches). The one in the bottom left is Japanese.

COLOUR CHANGERS

Devices added to luminaires to allow for the filter to be changed by remote control include:

1. The colour wheel which rotates in front of the unit putting any one of five colours into the light.
2. The semaphore that holds a filter like a flag in front of the unit. Any one of five colours or no colour, plus any combination can be in use at any one time.
3. The scroller that holds a roll of filters which crosses the unit on to another spool. Can hold up to thirty-two colours or more depending on make (*see* Fig. 87).

(*See also* Intelligent Luminaires, page 123.)

fairly complicated devices to allow a single unit to change colour (*see* above).

THE NATURE OF LIGHT

In the wide band of electromagnetic waves the only visible waves occupy a narrow span – from about 400–700 nanometres.

White light (daylight) is made up of an even amount of all of the visible spectrum.

All objects are reflectors, absorbers or transmitters of one or more colours.

There is no colour without light.

There are three factors involved in the perception of colour – the light source, the object lit, and the eye.

EXERCISE 21
NAMING COLOURS

This is an especially good exercise to carry out with two or more people.

One Person Version
a. Write down as many colours as you can name.
b. When you run out of ideas read the exercise analysis and see if it helps you think of some more.
c. When you next come to a halt read the list that follows the analysis and see how many you have missed.

More than One Person Version
a. Take it in turn to call out the name of a colour, with either one or all of you making a note of what has already been said.
b. Each person has three 'lives' and loses one when they fail to think of a colour.
c. After three lives are gone the person is 'out'.
d. The last person 'in' wins. Check your list against the list that follows the exercise analysis.

Analysis – Exercise 21
The human eye can identify many different shades of colour and probably all of them have been named at one time or another. However, you must now ask yourself what constitutes a colour and what does not. Red, for example, is clearly a colour. So perhaps is tangerine

and plum, but is tomato? Or is this simply another way of saying red? This is perhaps more in the realm of semantics than lighting. After all, plum may be considered a shade of purple or blue, as tangerine is a shade of orange. But can you see in your mind's eye a difference between orange and tangerine? Gold and silver are colours, but what of copper or bronze? Is ebony a colour? What about ruby or emerald?

Perhaps the test would be that if we were shown a chart containing all possible variations of colour and were asked to name one, we could do so more or less straight away because we know exactly what colour the name suggests. But even then no two individuals would necessarily agree, even on fairly basic colours. There is, for example, usually quite a lot of disagreement about the definition of purple, mauve and violet.

Colours (in Alphabetical Order)

* Almond, Amber, Apple, Apricot, Aquamarine, Ash, Auburn, Avocado, Azure,

* Bamboo, Banana, Barley, Beige, Bile, Black, Blonde, Blood, Blue, Bottle, Brick, Bronze, Brown, Burgundy, Buttercup, Butterscotch,

* Cadmium, Caramel, Carmine, Cerise, Cerulean, Champagne, Charcoal,

Derwent Watercolour • Derwent Studio
Colour Range • Gamme Couleurs • Farbaüfstellung

No	Colour	No	Colour	No	Colour
01	Zinc Yellow	25	Dark Violet	49	Sap Green
02	Lemon Cadmium	26	Light Violet	50	Cedar Green
03	Gold	27	Blue Violet Lake	51	Olive Green
04	Primrose Yellow	28	Delft Blue	52	Bronze
05	Straw Yellow	29	Ultramarine	53	Sepia
06	Deep Cadmium	30	Smalt Blue	54	Burnt umber
07	Naples Yellow	31	Cobalt Blue	55	Vandyke Brown
08	Middle Chrome	32	Spectrum Blue	56	Raw Umber
09	Deep Chrome	33	Light Blue	57	Brown Ochre
10	Orange Chrome	34	Sky Blue	58	Raw Sienna
11	Spectrum Orange	35	Prussian Blue	59	Golden Brown
12	Scarlet Lake	36	Indigo	60	Burnt Yellow Ochre
13	Pale Vermilion	37	Oriental Blue	61	Copper Beech
14	Deep Vermilion	38	Kingfisher Blue	62	Burnt Sienna
15	Geranium Lake	39	Turquoise Blue	63	Venetian Red
16	Flesh Pink	40	Turquoise Green	64	Terracotta
17	Pink Madder Lake	41	Jade Green	65	Burnt Carmine
18	Rose Pink	42	Juniper Green	66	Chocolate
19	Madder Carmine	43	Bottle Green	67	Ivory Black

*Fig. 40
Manufacturer's
paint chart.*

Cherry, Chestnut, Chocolate, Chrome, Claret, Coffee, Conker, Copper, Coral, Cream, Crimson, Cyan,
* Denim,
* Eau de Nile, Ecru, Eggshell, Emerald, Eucalyptus,
* Fawn, Fern, Flesh, Fuschia,
* Gamboge, Ginger, Gold, Grape, Grass, Green, Grey, Gunmetal,
* Haematite, Hazel, Honey,
* Indigo, Ivory,
* Jade, Jonquil,
* Khaki,
* Lavender, Lemon, Lilac, Lime,
* Madder, Magenta, Magnolia, Mahogany, Maroon, Mauve, Mint, Mushroom, Mustard,
* Navy, Nut,
* Oak, Ochre, Olive, Opal, Orange, Oyster,
* Parchment, Pea, Peach, Pearl, Pine, Pink, Platinum, Plum, Poppy, Primrose, Prussian, Puce, Purple,
* Quartz,
* Raspberry, Red, Rose, Ruby, Russet, Rust,
* Saffron, Sage, Salmon, Sapphire, Scarlet, Sepia, Sienna, Silver, Slate, Straw, Strawberry,
* Tan, Tangerine, Taupe, Teak, Terracotta, Titian, Toffee, Tomato, Turquoise,
* Umber, Ultramarine,
* Vanilla, Verdigris, Vermilion, Violet, Viridian,
* Walnut, Wheat, White, Wine,
* Yellow,
* Zinnia.

The next two exercises continue to explore what we think and feel about colour.

EXERCISE 22
FINDING COLOURS

Make you own colour chart by cutting out from old magazines a square inch of colour that you think defines each of the named colours in the list above. This may also prove to be a useful tool for later creative design work.

Analysis – Exercise 22

Although we all see colour in the same way (apart from the few of us who are colour-blind) no two people will agree on the same precise colour matched to the list. Perhaps this is partly because from birth we begin to decide which colours we like and which we do not like. We also tend to link colour to emotion. For example, we say green is for envy. Even a single colour as ordinary as white can evoke many different images. Look at the passage below from the excellent novel *Postcards* by E. Annie Proulx:

> In the garden Kosti and Paula threw sheets over the tomato plants to protect them from the night frost, old sheets Paula's mother had given her years ago, and patched in all hues of white, marble, ivory, milk-silver, snow, chalk, pearl, birchbark, ghost, moonflower, cloud, ash, quartz. The

teeth of autumn gnawed at the light. They trampled back and forth over the silvered clods, working together, the only ones left on the mountain farm now.

This passage is used again as the basis for a creative exercise in the use of colour (*see* Exercise 30, page 79).

EXERCISE 23
EMOTIONAL COLOUR

This exercise further tests our imagination in relation to colour. It relies on our linking of colour to emotion. Again this exercise works better with more than one person.

One Person Version
a. Cover the list above right with a piece of paper.
b. Reveal each one in turn and make a quick emotional response as to what colour the idea suggests to you.

More than One Person Version
a. Have one person read out the list whilst the others write down their colour responses.
b. The responses have to be made quickly.
c. Having completed the exercise read through the list again and compare responses.
d. Have a go at adding to the list and trying it on the rest of the group.

Envy   = green
Love   =
Peace   =
Hate   =
War   =
Lust   =
Greed   =
Passion =
Pain   =
Energy   =
Infinity =
Jealousy =
Death   =
Ecstasy =

and finally, what colour are

YOU   =

Analysis – Exercise 23
The first few concepts are easy, the later ones quite difficult. Much depends on our preconceived ideas and general life experience. If you have to think too long about an answer then it is probably the case that you do not really have one. In a group of people there can be some surprising differences of opinion. People can have quite aggressive likes and dislikes for certain colours, in fact a whole industry has grown up around the psychology of colour (*see* Bibliography).

EXERCISE 24
THE SPECTRUM

White light can be divided into the many colours of the spectrum. To prove this we will allow white light to pass through a prism. This exercise repeats the experiment first carried out by Sir Isaac Newton in 1704 (*see* Fig. 41).

Analysis – Exercise 24

Each wavelength band between 400–700nm (nanometres) is perceived by the normal eye as a spectral colour. The six main bands of spectral colour are:

400nm	Violet
	Blue
500nm	Green
600nm	Yellow
	Orange
700nm	Red

These are usually grouped into the three primary colours of light:

RAINBOW COLOURS

A rainbow is formed when raindrops act as prisms to split white light.

Defining each colour as it blends in with the one next to it has long caused problems. Newton himself repeatedly changed his mind during the course of his career, probably only choosing seven as an analogy with the musical octave.

400–500nm	Blue
500–600nm	Green
600–700nm	Red

Coloured light affects us emotionally and also affects what we see around us by changing the way it looks. The next two exercises examine this.

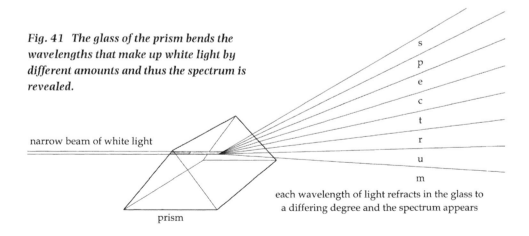

Fig. 41 *The glass of the prism bends the wavelengths that make up white light by different amounts and thus the spectrum is revealed.*

narrow beam of white light

s
p
e
c
t
r
u
m

prism

each wavelength of light refracts in the glass to a differing degree and the spectrum appears

EXERCISE 25
THE PRIMARY COLOURS

This exercise reverses the process and uses the primaries to create white light.

COLOUR FILTERS

Once made from gelatine, hence also known as gel. Most luminaires require a gel frame to hold the colour in place in front of the unit.

Many manufacturers specialize in making a wide range of colours for stage use, amongst them Strand, Lee, Rosco, Gelatran, and GAM. They offer swatch books of gel samples for ease of use (*see* Fig. 39).

Part 1

a. Using three good profile units (possibly with the aid of irises) and a screen or white wall create Fig. 42 as shown. You may also get a reasonable, if less precise result, using other luminaire types such as a fresnel or PC.

b. From what you see fill in the missing labels in Fig. 42.

Part 2

Use a variety of diffusion and neutral density gels on top of your focused colours, and note the different effects.

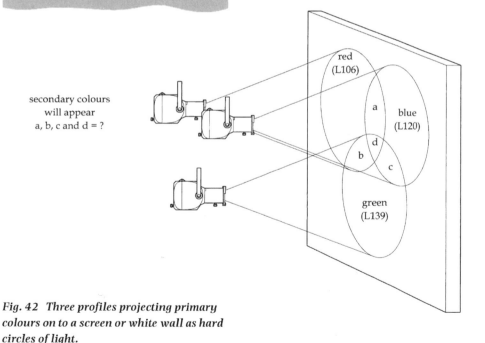

Fig. 42 Three profiles projecting primary colours on to a screen or white wall as hard circles of light.

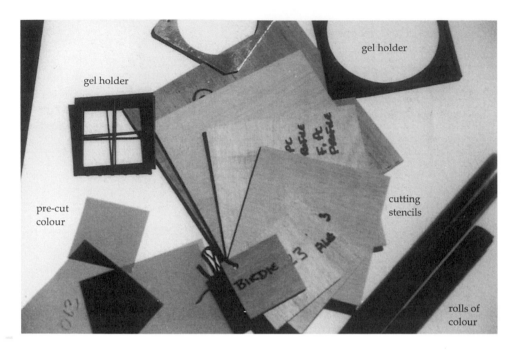

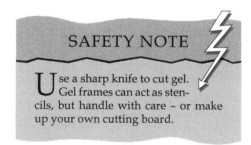

Fig. 43 Gel, gel frames and cutting templates.

SPECIAL FILTERS

The manufacturers of colour also produce filters that affect the light output in different ways:

1. Diffusion (also called frost) – this has the effect of diffusing the light output by softening the edges of a beam and is especially good for blending beams together.
2. Directional Diffusion (also called silk, or brushed silk) – this has the effect of diffusing a beam along one axis only. Especially useful for covering very tall or very wide areas.
3. Neutral Density – filters that reduce the light output but do not change the colour. The reduction is measured in photographic stops.

SAFETY NOTE

Use a sharp knife to cut gel. Gel frames can act as stencils, but handle with care – or make up your own cutting board.

Analysis – Exercise 25

The primary colours themselves mix to make the secondary colours. In Fig. 42:

a = Magenta (Red + Blue);
b = Yellow (Red + Green);
c = Cyan (Blue + Green); d = White.

LABELLING GEL

A wax pencil or chinagraph can be used to mark the number of the colour on to the gel so it can be easily identified. The number will not appear as an image in the light as it is well out of the focal point of the beam.

DICHROIC COLOUR

A number of sophisticated lighting instruments, such as the Vari-lite, create colour dichroically. Each unit uses filters that work by reflecting unwanted parts of the spectrum rather than absorbing them like traditional filters. This allows for greater transmission of light and cooler running of the instrument.

TRANSMISSION OF LIGHT THROUGH GEL

Transmission of light through colour filters can be shown as a graph which shows the amount and scope of the wavelengths allowed through the medium (*see* Fig. 44).

The percentage figure for transmission is given thus: Y = 23 per cent.

Colour is created by the transmission of light through a colour filter. This absorbs certain wavelengths of light and transmits others, thus a colour is produced. A filter approximating to a primary colour will only let through one third of white light. A side effect of this absorption is heat (*see* Fig. 44).

EXERCISE 26
ADDITIVE COLOUR MIXING

This exercise uses the rig from Exercise 25 as in Fig. 42.

a. Refocus the three primary colours onto one spot.
b. By changing the levels of the three primaries create the following colours:

White
Orange
Sky-Blue
Pink
Magenta
Brown
Grey

Analysis – Exercise 26

Additive colour mixing occurs when more than one light source is lighting a common object and each source uses a different filter. This type of colour mixing is very widely used on stage – in fact it is almost impossible not to use it! Each different colour used in the luminaires adds to the range of visible light. Additive colour mixing thus tends

COLOUR AND LIGHT

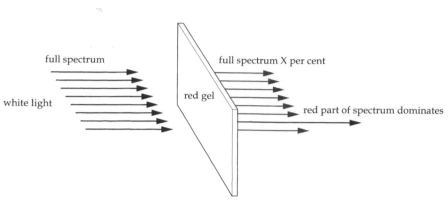

A certain amount of white light is transmitted (X per cent) but more in the RED part of the spectrum. The greater X per cent the paler the colour. If X per cent = 0 the colour is said to be SATURATED.

TRANSMISSION GRAPHS

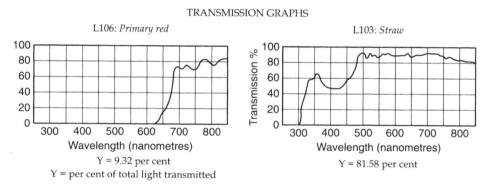

Y = per cent of total light transmitted

Fig. 44 The creation of colour by transmission of light through a filter (above) and manufacturers' transmission graphs,

towards the creation of white light. This exercise rather depends on the purity or efficiency of your luminaires. It is not easy to get a perfect result as most luminaires are not manufactured to act as efficient projectors. However, even if the overall coverage is a bit patchy you should find white created somewhere in your picture. You will find however that it will not be pro-duced with all your units at the same level – blue gel usually transmits less light than the others and will therefore have to be quite a bit brighter than the other two.

The earlier colours in the list should generally have proved no problem: orange is red and yellow, sky-blue is blue with green, pink is red and blue, magenta a secondary mix of red and

DARK COLOURS

Transmission of light through very dark colours is rather poor – for primary blue it is only approximately 6 per cent.

Dark colours cause a luminaire to give out quite low levels of light. By absorbing so much of the light the gel gets hotter and disintegrates quicker, and so needs to be renewed more frequently.

blue. Brown and grey may have proved more difficult – they are best found by using very low light levels as they are colours made through the darkening of shades. Black is the one colour we cannot make – except by turning off all of the units!

EXERCISE 27
PERCEPTION OF
LIGHT AND COLOUR

This exercise continues to explore additive colour mixing. Again, use the rig from Exercise 25 but initially without the screen. Focus onto one spot (as described in Exercise 26), where we are going to place some objects.

Part 1
a. Choose a range of colourful objects, some of a single colour, some multi-coloured.
b. Put each item in front of each primary in turn and note how the colour of the object appears to change.

Part 2
a. Replace the screen.
b. Re-create your white light by mixing all three primaries.
c. Hold an object or your hand in front of the screen and note the shadows that are cast.
d. To further your understanding of what you are seeing answer the following question: Which unit, with which colour in, is casting the yellow shadow?

Analysis – Exercise 27

Part I
This exercise will depend a lot on the objects you have chosen to place in the light. An object is dependent for colour upon the kind of light that strikes it. All objects except light sources are reflectors. A surface that is normally white in daylight becomes red when lit by a red light, green in green light, and so on. An article that is red in daylight appears black when lit by a green light because green light does not contain the one colour, red, that can be reflected from the object.

A *rough* surface will reflect more light of all wavelengths than a *smooth* surface of the same colour. Hence colour darkens with a surface that is polished, wet, oily, or has a large fibre size, and lightens with a surface that is rough, dry or powdered, or has a small fibre size. Some surfaces such as oil or mother-of-pearl have a more dramatic effect on light as they reflect the spectrum in a particular way.

If you have used a good range of coloured objects, amongst other things, you should find:

1. Green light makes red turn black and vice versa.
2. Under a primary colour an object with the same colour and white will look all-white. For example, a red and white striped sweater will look completely white under a red light.
3. Many blues have some red in them and vice versa.
4. If you look at an object in a single saturated colour the brain appears to redefine that as white light, in other words, despite knowing that you are looking at red light a white object will continue to look white.
5. After looking at one colour long enough the sudden absence of it stimulates the eye to see the opposite complimentary colour.

Part 2

The multicoloured shadows created in this exercise demonstrate once again the creation of secondary colours through the combination of two primaries. Thus it is the shadow cast by the unit containing the blue primary that gets lit with the mix of the red and the green units to make yellow. This also goes to demonstrate why colours are not mixed on stage in this way. Using the primaries at various levels would allow for any colour to be created, but this only really works on a flat plane like the screen, or the back wall of a stage – the cyclorama. In three dimensions the effect is decidedly psychedelic. We have also noted that the use of dark colours means a subsequent loss of light output (*see* box on previous page).

A whole different range of colours can be derived from subtractive colour mixing as the next exercise demonstrates.

EXERCISE 28
SUBTRACTIVE COLOUR MIXING

Rig a single unit and project it on to the screen, then carry out the following:

Part 1
a. Put one primary colour into the unit and then add another.
b. Add the final primary to complete the effect.
c. Try the primaries in another order to see if the effect is different.

Part 2
a. Use a range of lighter filters adding two or three together in the unit at one time.
b. Try and predict what colour will

The best way to see the colour a filter is going to make before putting it into a unit is to look through a sample at a light source similar to that of the unit (*see* Colour Changers, page 66, *see also* Definitions of White Light, page 82).

come from the mixture before using it.

c. Think of a reasonably dark colour and try to make it by mixing two lighter colours together.

d. Does the order in which the colours are added make any difference?

e. Try two pieces of the same colour – what happens then?

Analysis – Exercise 28

Subtractive colour mixing occurs when more than one filter is used in the same instrument, usually each of a different colour and one on top of the other. Each filter reduces the scope of the colour transmitted from the instrument. Subtractive colour mixing tends towards the absence of any light.

Part 1

In fact, even two primaries, rather than three, cut out almost all of the light output from the luminaire, and the order makes no difference.

Part 2

Subtractive mixing is of use when we want to use a colour that we cannot find in the manufacturer's range. By mixing two colours we create a new one. The order in which we put them into the unit makes no difference, they will both act separately on the light source allowing only a certain range of colour to be transmitted.

One might predict therefore that using two pieces of the same colour would be no different to using just one piece as they are acting on the same part of the colour range, but this is not so. This is because most colour filters allow a certain amount of white light to be transmitted. By using two filters of the same colour the amount of this white light is reduced so less gets through and thus a more 'saturated' colour appears – a kind of thicker version of the original colour (*see* information box, page 78). Of all subtractive colour mixing it is this that the lighting designer makes most use of. In a similar way, a colour can be slightly lightened by cutting small holes in the gel to allow some extra white light to be transmitted (*see* Fig. 45).

EXERCISE 29
SPLIT COLOURS

Colour can be used in one other way within a luminaire. A split colour is when gels are placed beside each other

COLOUR AND LIGHT

USING SPLIT GEL

Split gels are usually of two, up to a maximum of four pieces. The pieces of the gel are usually held in place well enough by the gel frame, but a special adhesive tape is available for extra security.

ADDITIVE: Gel 1+Gel 2 = colour 3

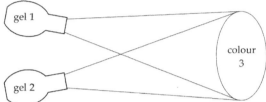

G1 = RED; G2 = GREEN; C3 = YELLOW
ADDITIVE COLOUR MIXING TENDS TOWARDS WHITE

SUBTRACTIVE: Gel 1–Gel 2 = colour 3

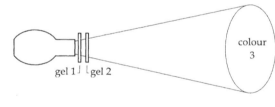

G1 = RED; G2 = GREEN; C3 = YELLOW
SUBTRACTIVE COLOUR MIXING TENDS TOWARDS BLACK

If gel 1 and gel 2 are the same colour (e.g. both L103 *Straw*) the resultant colour 3 is a darker version of L103 as the percentage of white light transmission is reduced (*see* Fig. 44). Likewise if holes are cut in the gel a greater per cent of white light will be transmitted and the colour lightened.

Fig. 45 Colour mixing in light.

in the same gel frame. Strictly speaking, this is not colour mixing, but nevertheless it can produce a great effect. Try it with the following exercise:

a. Use the lighting rig from Exercise 25.
b. Make up a split colour using two of the primaries and try it in one of the units. See what difference focusing the luminaire makes.
c. Next try the same thing using a three-way split using the three primaries.
d. Make one final split for the third unit of your own choosing.
e. Finally choose three different gobos and add them to the rig. Test out

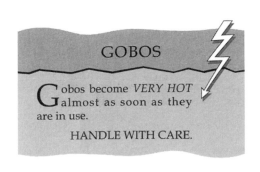

GOBOS

Gobos become *VERY HOT* almost as soon as they are in use.

HANDLE WITH CARE.

various focuses and combinations of the three units.

Analysis – Exercise 29

With split colour the focus of the lantern allows for the single colours to be seen in the beam as well as the resultant additive mix. However, the gel is not near the focal point of the unit and therefore it is impossible to focus clearly between the two colours, so you cannot make pictures by simply drawing on the gel.

For the same reason it is not possible to locate colour to specific parts of a gobo, although colour gobos are now produced. A gobo image like a stained-glass window is created by using several gobos in different luminaries, each with a different colour. These are called composite gobos.

Split colour works particularly well in combination with gobos and is commonly used to suggest such scenes as a leafy glade (by splitting greens), or sunlight through leaves (by splitting yellows) (*see* Fig. 46).

Finally in this chapter, an exercise that allows for some artistic experimentation with colour.

EXERCISE 30
PLAYING WITH COLOUR

Use the extract from the novel *Postcards* by E. Annie Proulx on page 68 to create a patchwork of colours suggested by the passage. Use any equipment and colour you wish but light on to a white, flat surface such as a wall or screen.

Analysis – Exercise 30

Partly this is an exercise in restraint. In this chapter we have been mainly using the primaries and other dark colours to explore the world of colour, but in fact on stage it is the lighter hues and tones that give the subtlest scope. The whites and off-whites suggested by the passage have provided the scope for you to create a piece with subtly different but similar shades. However, there is no right answer and perhaps this project can also be resolved by using the brightest hues – who is to say?

SUMMARY

In using colour, restraint is often necessary, and it is the whiter shades that we will examine in the next chapter which deals with how the lighting designer recreates the colour of sunlight on stage.

BREAKUPS

Triangles (small)

Multi Coils

Shapes Breakup 2

Matrix

Holes

FOLIAGE BREAKUPS

Bamboo Leaves

Jungle Leaf

Jungle Leaves

Ferns

Fir Cones

WINDOWS

Street Window

Victorian

French Windows

French Doors

French Doors 2

CLOUDS

Cloud 11

Cloud 12

Clouds (Distorted)

Childish Clouds

Cloud Outlines

MESHTONE CLOUDS

Nimbus

Cumulo Nimbus 1

Cumulo Nimbus 2

Cumulo Nimbus 3

Strato Cumulus

GLASS

Moon Glass

Cumulus Glass

Cirrus Glass

Nimbus Glass

COMPOSITE

Stained Glass
(Green)

Stained Glass
(Yellow)

Stained Glass
(Blue)

Stained Glass
(Red)

Stained Glass
(White)

7

MAKING IT LOOK REAL

'It Is the East, and Juliet Is the sun'

This chapter explores the lighter tints and hues in the gel range, in particular the colour of sunlight. We start by examining the concept of 'white light', light with no artificially added colour medium.

Fig. 46 Manufactured gobos. A typical selection from DHA Ltd (Opposite page).

Fig. 47 A sunlit scene – the real thing.

OPEN WHITE

An open white luminaire, one that has no colour fitted, is marked o/w on a lighting design plan. Thus we know that an unmarked unit on a plan represents an error, and a gel is missing from the list.

A luminaire with no gel is usually described as being 'open white'. But is an open white luminaire the same colour as sunlight? How could it be when we know that at different times of day (or year) sunlight itself appears differently coloured? What about the electric light in our homes, a fluorescent light, or even candlelight?

You should know from your own experience that these light sources radiate different colours, although admittedly occupying a small range of whitish hues. These colours are described, and differ from each other, by appearing to us to emit 'colder' (light blue), or 'warmer' (very light orange) light.

The next exercise should help further clarify this concept.

EXERCISE 31
WHITE LIGHT

Part 1

Look at the following list of white light sources and put them in order of warmth. Start with the source you think gives the warmest white light and finish with the coldest.

1. Warm fluorescent light

2. Summer sunlight

3. A 1,000 watt tungsten halogen bulb

4. Winter sunlight

5. A candle

6. Cold fluorescent light

7. A 40 watt bulb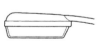

8. An overcast sky

9. A sodium street light

10. A 150 watt bulb

Part 2

Do you think some of the light sources are closer to each other than others? Go back to your list and group the sources in this way. You may think the candlelight is almost the same as a 40 watt bulb, and that a 1,000 watt bulb is very much brighter than sunlight – show this on your list.

Analysis – Exercise 31

The correct order of light sources is shown in Fig. 48. The correct name for this concept of the appearance of light sources is 'colour temperature' (CT). It is measured in degrees kelvin (K). Colour temperature was developed in order to standardize the measurement of the spectral content of white light. The colour is identified with reference to the heating up of a physical object. In effect the object will move from black through orange, to red hot, to white hot as the temperature increases. Thus a warm, or high orange-

COLOUR TEMPERATURE FILTERS

Various filters are manufactured to alter the colour temperature from one light source to another, for example L201 converts tungsten to daylight, from 3,200°K to 5,700°K.

These can also be used to line up the CT of units that use different light sources (*see* Discharge Units, page 42).

content source like a candle has a *low* CT, whilst a cold, brighter source like northern sunlight has a *high* CT. Colour temperature is a measurement of the appearance of the light, not the amount, although it can be noted that duller sources tend to have a lower CT.

EXERCISE 32
COLOUR TEMPERATURE

Part 1

a. Rig two identical luminaires (preferably of about 1,000 watts) and focus them at any reasonably large, familiar object.

b. Dim one of the units and note if the CT changes.

Part 2

a. Put both units at full.

b. Leaving one unit o/w, put a CT gel in the second unit that converts tungsten to daylight (in Lee Filters, for example, this is L201).

c. Note the difference in colour.

d. Look hard at the colour coming from the CT unit and then look out of a window to compare it with sunlight. If you can open a window or door in your working space to make a direct comparison, so much the better, even the smallest of cracks of light will do.

e. Repeat the experiment with the gel meant to correct tungsten to fluorescent light – comparing with both the non-gelled unit and a real fluorescent light.

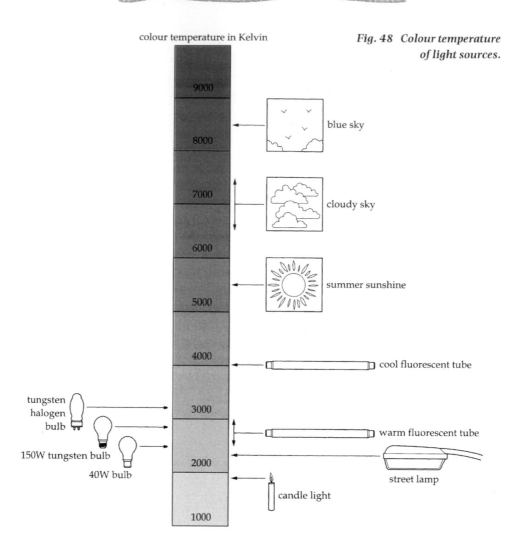

colour temperature in Kelvin

Fig. 48 Colour temperature of light sources.

9000

8000 — blue sky

7000 — cloudy sky

6000

5000 — summer sunshine

4000 — cool fluorescent tube

tungsten halogen bulb — 3000 — warm fluorescent tube

150W tungsten bulb — street lamp

40W bulb — 2000

candle light

1000

f. Repeat with as many CT gels as possible.

Analysis – Exercise 32

It is surprising how blue the CT converter to sunlight is. In our theatre spaces we somehow accept a much warmer source as being white light without really

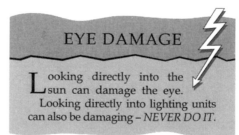

EYE DAMAGE

Looking directly into the sun can damage the eye. Looking directly into lighting units can also be damaging – *NEVER DO IT.*

noticing that it has any colour. The very dimming of a unit warms its CT (Part 1 in the exercise), and therefore will also affect the way it projects a filter colour. (Remember from the CT diagram that a 40 watt bulb had a lower CT than a 150 watt bulb.)

Whilst it may be possible to create the correct colour temperature of a given light source using CT filters, it is sometimes better to use a colour that is more true to the way in which the viewer *thinks* of the world rather than the way it really *is*. In this way one might use a warmer straw gel for a hot summer's day rather than the more accurate bluish CT colour.

All the CT filters should be thought of as colours in their own right and as important additions to the filter range available to the lighting designer. It is also important that the lighting designer does not regard using no gel as something particularly special, but simply as another colour option.

Let us now apply this to the creation of a sunlit scene.

EXERCISE 33
THE COLOUR OF DAYLIGHT

Part 1
a. Place your subject on a chair, face front.
b. Rig as many luminaires as you think you will need to create the look of the sun shining on your actor on a hot sunny day. (Remember what you learnt about lighting angles and key light in Chapter 5.)
c. If you are not sure how to approach this exercise in terms of choosing luminaire positions, you may consider using part or all of the lighting rig from Exercise 15 as illustrated in Fig. 31.
d. Take your time to choose whatever colours you think are needed to put into your rig to create the effect of a hot sunny day.
e. Looking at your finished state, answer the following questions:

   1. If a director asked for this hot and sunny scene to look even warmer could you effectively alter the colour to achieve this?
   2. Could you take out any single luminaire and retain the overall effect?
   3. Could you use the same rig and by simply changing levels suggest the sun is elsewhere?

f. Without telling them what you have been trying to achieve, ask someone to look at your lighting and describe what they think of the quality of the light.

Part 2
a. When you are happy with the way your state looks simply replace your colours with a new set of gels to change the mood to that of a cold winter's day.

b. Looking at your finished state, answer the following questions:

1. In changing your colours how much 'bluer' did you go? What would you have chosen to suggest an even colder day – say at the North Pole?
2. Which state do you prefer – warm or cold?
3. What makes you like one more than the other?

Analysis – Exercise 33

To complete this exercise successfully you will have carried out the following:

1. Selected an angle as key light to suggest your sun, and made this the brightest.
2. Made sure the rest of the rig complemented this key source – no competing strong angles.
3. Your colour choice should have been warm but not too outrageous, it is important that that no 'colour' as such should be read by the audience.

Fig. 49 illustrates possible solutions.

The first point to note in this exercise is that in the dark theatre space a single luminaire will not suffice to create the effect of sunlight: a single directional source will create too strong a set of shadows. Other units are required to duplicate the work done in real life by objects and the atmosphere around us that reflect and diffuse sunlight.

The purpose of the exercise is to make sure you have thought through your choices carefully. If you could not possibly conceive of using a warmer set of gels for the summer's day, then what would you use for tropical or desert heat? You need to develop your own range of colour choices which will allow you flexibility, and somewhere else to go if required.

You will possibly have come across the problem of context. Anybody looking at the actor may well have had a problem seeing that sunlight was your intention because the actor is probably sitting in an otherwise darkened room and therefore has no context. In a full stage production this will not be such a problem. In these exercises it simply means that the viewer

SUNLIGHT

A special kind of reflection phenomenon, called scattering, underlies the colour we see in the sky. If there was nothing in the atmosphere, no dust or gases, the sky would appear black – as it does in space. However when sunlight passes through the atmosphere, molecules of various gases scatter the light. Because they scatter the short wavelengths more (the blue end of the spectrum) the sky takes on a blue hue and the sun appears yellow.

When there is more dust or moisture in the air these particles act to scatter the longer wavelengths as well as the shorter ones and the sky becomes whiter.

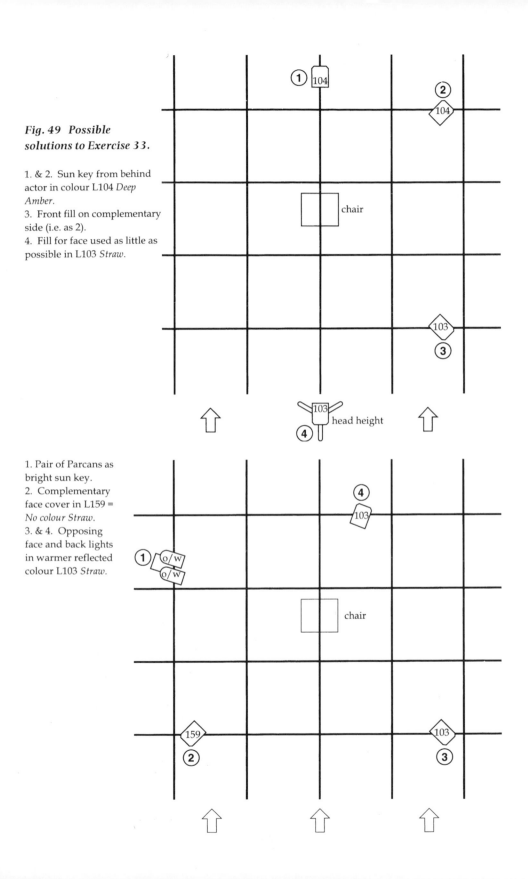

Fig. 49 Possible solutions to Exercise 33.

1. & 2. Sun key from behind actor in colour L104 *Deep Amber*.
3. Front fill on complementary side (i.e. as 2).
4. Fill for face used as little as possible in L103 *Straw*.

1. Pair of Parcans as bright sun key.
2. Complementary face cover in L159 = *No colour Straw*.
3. & 4. Opposing face and back lights in warmer reflected colour L103 *Straw*.

must concentrate on the object lit and not on the surrounding area. Admittedly this is not always easy.

Hopefully you will also have made a mental note about the success or otherwise of your colour choice, noting the manufacturer's name and gel number for future reference. These colours will be the start of an understanding of the full colour range which will grow as you use more and more colour in ever differing contexts.

A final exercise in this chapter – again similar to the previous two.

EXERCISE 34
SUNSET/MOONRISE

Rig the equipment to create the appearance of the following on your subject:

a. Sunset
b. Moonlight

Analysis – Exercise 34

Your lighting state should have involved a rig giving a specific key source with colouring to suggest the nature of that source. Other luminaires used to complete the picture should be coloured to complement and support the source whilst not detracting from it.

With the *sunset* a low angle is required. Although it is usually the sky rather than the fading sun that appears orange at sunset, it is a theatre lighting cliché that the audience expectation of the nature of sunlight at sunset is more romantic than the reality. Therefore a much warmer colour than we would usually consider for sunlight, such as a dark orange or even red gel, is as acceptable as a more realistic choice of colour. Again it is a matter of personal preference and dramatic context.

Another example of audience expectation is in the difference between sunrise and sunset. What colour changes would you have made to the exercise above if it had been to create a sunrise rather than a sunset? The coloration we see in a sunrise or sunset is caused by the sun shining through a greater layer of the earth's atmosphere to reach us. In piercing an even greater degree of dust/moisture the longer wavelengths of light are scattered more than normal and the sky appears more orange or red.

As the same applies to either the sun rising or setting, the same colours can be seen in either event. Perhaps the heat of the day gives rise to a likelihood of more particles being in the air at sunset and thus we more often witness the phenomenon then – or perhaps we are just more likely to catch the sunset rather than be up for sunrise. Either way, people tend to have greater expectations of sunset than sunrise, tending to feel that the former is likely to be more spectacular – 'redder', whilst sunrise is cooler – blue or pink. As always you have to make up your own mind.

For *moonlight*, a light blue is usually the colour most people would choose. Yet once again a range of colours are

Fig. 50 Sunset.

(Below) *Fig. 51 Moonlight.*

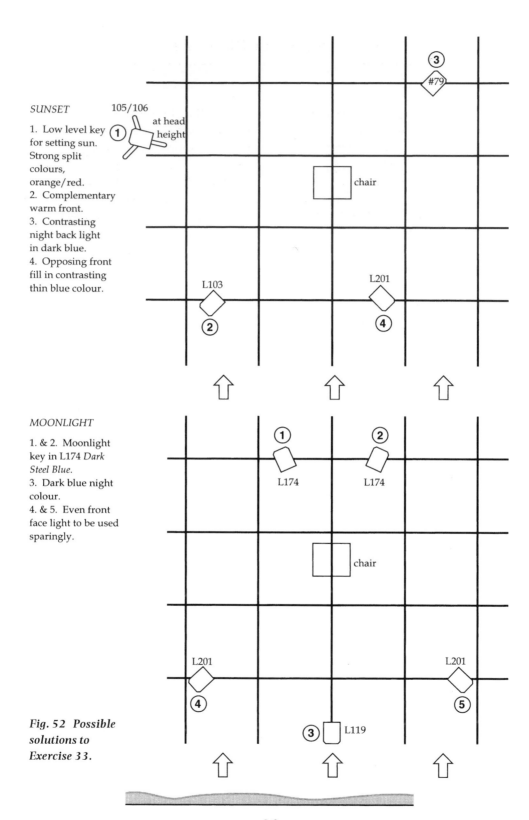

SUNSET   105/106

1. Low level key ① for setting sun. Strong split colours, orange/red.
2. Complementary warm front.
3. Contrasting night back light in dark blue.
4. Opposing front fill in contrasting thin blue colour.

at head height

chair

L103

L201

② ④

MOONLIGHT

1. & 2. Moonlight key in L174 _Dark Steel Blue_.
3. Dark blue night colour.
4. & 5. Even front face light to be used sparingly.

① ②

L174   L174

chair

L201   L201

④ ⑤

③ L119

Fig. 52 Possible solutions to Exercise 33.

90

conceivable to suggest harvest moons, blood moons, summer moons, winter moons, evil moons, waning and waxing moons, and so on. Night itself is also subject to wide interpretation. Alongside the moonlight you may have thought to create the 'rest' of the night, in other words a context for the moonlight. If so, a dark blue is often thought acceptable. However, this again is really more theatrical shorthand than a reflection of reality as most nights are dark rather than colourful but darkness does really not help us see the action on stage!

Fig. 52 illustrates some possible solutions.

SUMMARY

In this chapter you will also have created your first real lighting designs – lighting which creates the illusion of a real setting. Choice of equipment has been required: soft pools of light from fresnels, PCs or soft-focused profiles. Perhaps parcans, or even beam lights, were used for the source light. Key light played its part and lighting angles were further investigated. The need for a context for the lighting has been emphasized, and the likely expectations of the audience considered. In attempting to create realistic light we explored our own preconceptions and values, especially in terms of our chosen colours.

A final note about day and night settings. We know that often we see the moon in the sky during the day. Yet, when suggesting a setting to an audience, we require their immediate and unequivocal acknowledgement of our intentions. We need them to believe us straightaway. This being the case, I believe it is true to say that no lighting designer would ever place a day-moon in a daytime lighting state. Unless, that is, they positively wanted to confuse the issue. However bright and sunny the lighting state, with a moon gobo in the sky, the audience would simply think it was an exceptionally bright night, a stage convention, or a mistake!

Of course various locations on earth give rise to particular local air conditions and thus a particular look to the sky. For example, the abundance of water vapour around Venice (and parts of Italy generally) gives this area a famously bright blue radiance. The next chapter moves us closer to creating just such specific lighting locations, and looks at the textbook conventions on general cover.

GENERAL COVER

A body of luminaires rigged to cover a large part or all of the performing area, and specifically designed to give good actor visibility.

A general cover may be non-specific, and thus underlying the other lighting moods, or be very specific and the main mood-setter itself.

8

A GENERAL COVER OF LIGHT

'For Every Season There Is a Time'

GENERAL COVER

A 'general cover' is the technical application and expansion of what we have already discovered about lighting an object or person. Up to this point we have made lighting decisions based on our opinion of what works and what does not, aiming at creating strong and exciting lighting. We have learnt that the use of key light and especially back light greatly enhances the lighting picture and adds realism. The basic concept of a general cover is not that the light on stage needs to have any particular appearance or creative slant but simply that the performers on stage are visible. The light is believable, but does not need to make a comment of its own. As its name suggests, the light simply covers the stage in a general manner, and the performers are clearly visible over the entire acting area. The opposite concept to that of the general cover is the 'special'.

In practice, a general cover may make a vividly dynamic and exciting

THE SPECIAL

This is an individual unit placed in the design for use at a specific moment and usually covering a specific small area, for example, a single luminaire brought up on a solo actor for a monologue, soliloquy, or an aside.

A rig may have any number of 'specials'.

contribution to the stage lighting but, as the definition above implies, it does not have to. A basic general cover of light by its very nature underpins many a great lighting design.

The first exercise in this chapter demonstrates the underlying notion of the general cover.

EXERCISE 35
GENERAL COVER 1 –
COVERING THE STAGE

a. Within your working space mark out an area approximately 1 metre

FOCUSING

In all the practical exercises units will need to be rigged and focused. When working in small groups you may well focus your own equipment, but in a group it is worth practising using somebody else to focus for you as this is more usual in the theatre world. A few tips:

1. Direct the focuser clearly using direct and simple terms – 'bigger', 'smaller', 'to the left', 'up a bit', and so on.
2. Better still, be on stage and be specific – 'put the edge of the beam here', 'cut the beam off to this side here'.
3. Lighting designers often stand where they want the light to hit but be sure not to look into the units – as well as being bad for you, you will be unable to see clearly what you are doing for a few moments.
4. It helps to make the beam as small as possible to start with so that you can see clearly where it is.
5. Move out of the area to look at where the light is falling, or face away from the source and use your shadow as a guide.

(*See also* Focusing Practice, page 95.)

(or yard) deep by 5 metres (or yards) wide.

b. Place your point of view to face across the width of the working space.

c. In this area create lighting to suggest a bright spring day.

Analysis – Exercise 35

In this exercise the problem is how to light the stage so that it has uniformity across the width. Using a luminaire that will single-handedly cover such a wide area is one solution, but a wasteful or untidy one as the corresponding depth is not required and a lot of light will be wasted when shuttered off. This applies equally to front, back, top – any angle of light.

A better solution is to use a number of luminaires to allow for the width whilst also better containing the depth (*see* Fig. 54). In this solution we are using luminaires in groups to suggest the idea of a single light source. The result is neater than using larger, spreading units.

There is another advantage to doing this as the next exercise will demonstrate.

EXERCISE 36
GENERAL COVER 2 – COPYING REALITY

a. Rig a single profile and hard focus it across your theatre space to suggest light through a window. Use a gobo with a good number of sections if available.

b. Note how the sides of the window appear to diverge as they leave the luminaire, as do any other lines within the gobo.

c. If the weather permits, compare this with sunlight through a real window.

Fig. 53 General cover underpins the lighting in this dingy shot in Can't pay! Won't pay! *by Dario Fo.*

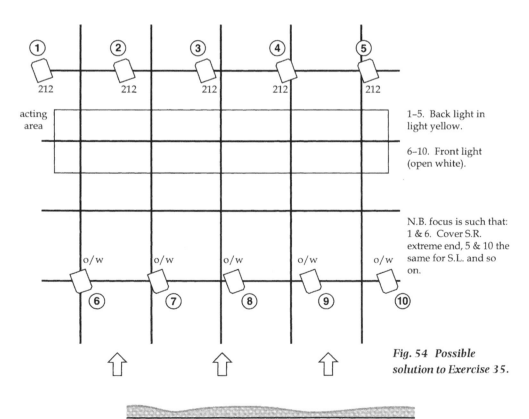

212   212   212   212   212

acting
area

o/w   o/w   o/w   o/w   o/w

1–5. Back light in
light yellow.

6–10. Front light
(open white).

N.B. focus is such that:
1 & 6. Cover S.R.
extreme end, 5 & 10 the
same for S.L. and so
on.

*Fig. 54 Possible
solution to Exercise 35.*

Light radiates from lightbulb in all directions. As we look at a person moving from a to b we are aware of the difference in appearance.

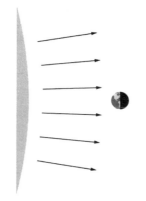

Light from the Sun radiates exactly as from the bulb above.

Because the Earth is so small the light arriving from the Sun appears to have no angle of divergence – i.e. as if parallel beams.

Fig. 55 Light coming from the sun to earth. Diverging light angles on stage, or from a lightbulb.

Analysis – Exercise 36

Real sunlight appears to exist as a source of parallel beams. This is because of the scale and distances involved between the earth and the sun (*see* Fig. 55).

When a general cover is required over a large area, the divergence of light from the units used can result in an unrealistic appearance, especially if we are trying to recreate daylight. As the diagram implies, a very large unit used to cover a large stage space simply causes the problem of a range of angles hitting the actor at different places on the set – some of which are not as good as others when lighting the face for clarity. Splitting the area into usable sections and lighting each one as if from the same direction allows for the continuity of the angle across the stage.

Naturally the area lights will be soft focused to blend into each other. This is something we shall practise in the next exercise.

EXERCISE 37
GENERAL COVER 3 – FOCUSING PRACTICE

a. Mark out an area that you would happily split into two or three distinct areas so that you can practice blending together parts of a general cover.

b. Decide on your audience point of view.

c. Light the area to create a general cover that appears to contain three distinctly different angles of light. If, for example, you are splitting into two areas you will need to rig six luminaires.

d. Colour each of the three angles with highly contrasting colours (perhaps to suggest a circus atmosphere) but also to more clearly delineate the angles in use.

Analysis – Exercise 37

In a general cover exercise such as this it is important to make sure the cover is fully comprehensive – that the corners and edges are lit as well as the centre of the stage. You should be looking for an even cover of light from each of the three angles. The units will be soft focused and the amount of overlap should be such that you have no gaps, dark spots between areas, or bright areas where the overlapping of two units occurs (see Fig. 56).

Focusing a good general cover takes a little practice but soon becomes second nature to a busy lighting designer. Getting an even general cover is probably one of the most difficult and yet most important skills that the lighting designer has to master.

The next exercise gives you further practice and is one stage more difficult.

EXERCISE 38
GENERAL COVER 4 – FURTHER PRACTICE

a. Mark out a reasonably sized one-unit area. Place inside it a short A-frame ladder and a chair (see Fig. 57).

b. Decide on your audience point of view.

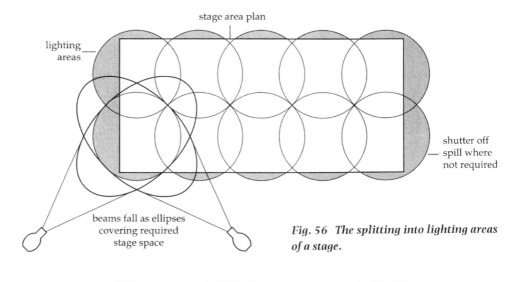

stage area plan

lighting areas

shutter off
spill where
not required

beams fall as ellipses
covering required
stage space

Fig. 56 The splitting into lighting areas of a stage.

MARK OUT

A mark out is the term used for the putting of lines (usually coloured PVC tape) on the rehearsal room floor to indicate the acting area of a set.

c. Light the area as in the previous exercise to create a general cover which appears to contain three distinctly different angles of light. You must light for an actor sitting on the chair, and climbing up to the third rung of the ladder. The cover must be even everywhere except under the ladder. (If you have not got a ladder, another chair or a table would do as long as you make provision for the actor to be lit standing on it.)

d. Colour each of the three angles with highly contrasting colours (in this case to suggest the landscape of a strange planet) and to more clearly delineate the angles in use.

Analysis – Exercise 38

This is a difficult general cover to get right with the height dimension and the ladder getting in the way. The trick here, as is often the case, is to start by making a good choice of angles. The lighting designer will often have the freedom to dictate where the source is

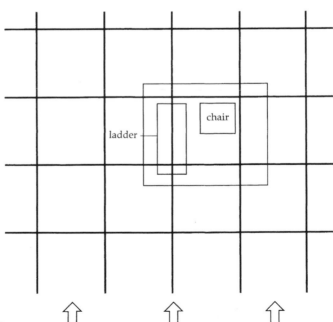

Fig. 57 Mark out of area with furniture (Exercise 38).

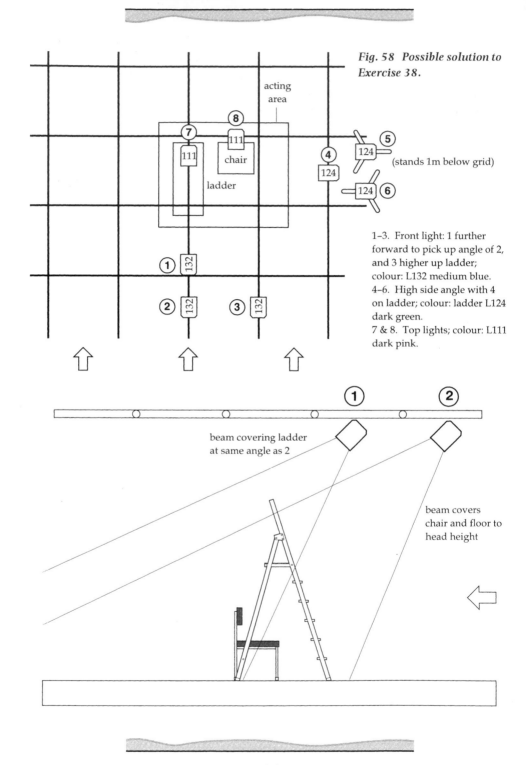

Fig. 58 Possible solution to Exercise 38.

acting area

(stands 1m below grid)

1–3. Front light: 1 further forward to pick up angle of 2, and 3 higher up ladder; colour: L132 medium blue.
4–6. High side angle with 4 on ladder; colour: ladder L124 dark green.
7 & 8. Top lights; colour: L111 dark pink.

beam covering ladder at same angle as 2

beam covers chair and floor to head height

coming from as the director or designer will rarely dictate the sun's position, for example. In order to make the lighting effective we should think carefully about what angles are going to be the most interesting and the most possible to achieve. Clearly there would be no point in choosing the most artistically creative angles if, after the units are rigged and the set built, they proved impossible to get back to for focusing! (*See* Fig. 58.)

EXERCISE 39
GENERAL COVER 5 – EXTERIORS

a. Choose, and adapt for your own working space, one of the four suggested acting area mark-outs as shown in the diagram below.

b. Create a piece of lighting within the area to suggest one of the following naturalistic settings, always remembering that the lighting must not only look right but also function correctly (that is, actor usability):

1. A forest glade on a sunny day.
2. A hot and parched desert.
3. A bleak, cold day in the Arctic Circle.
4. Night-time in a jungle.

c. Repeat the exercise as often as desired choosing a different mark-out and end-product from the list each time.

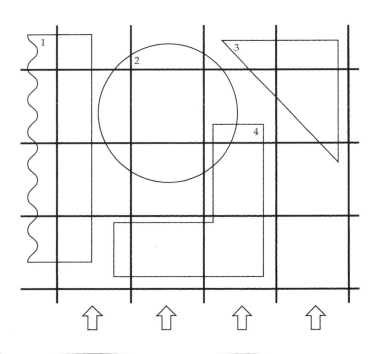

Fig. 59 Acting area plans for Exercise 39.

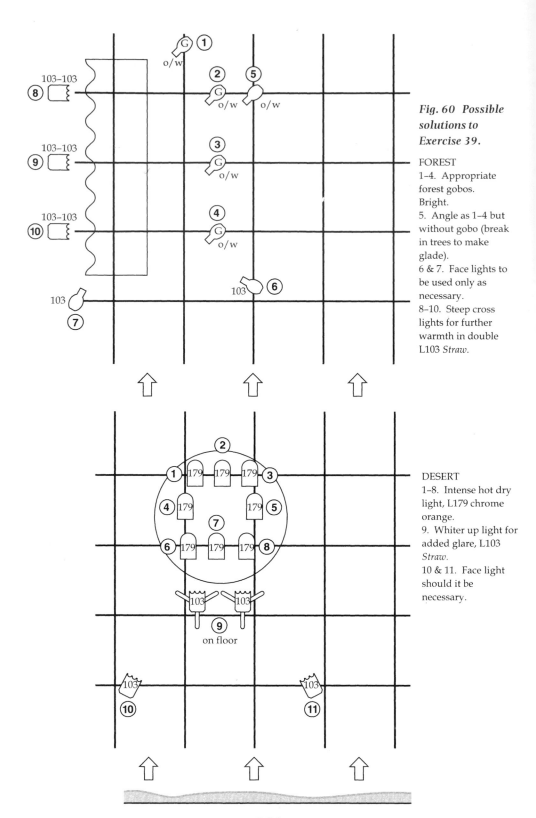

Fig. 60 Possible solutions to Exercise 39.

FOREST
1–4. Appropriate forest gobos. Bright.
5. Angle as 1–4 but without gobo (break in trees to make glade).
6 & 7. Face lights to be used only as necessary.
8–10. Steep cross lights for further warmth in double L103 *Straw*.

DESERT
1–8. Intense hot dry light, L179 chrome orange.
9. Whiter up light for added glare, L103 *Straw*.
10 & 11. Face light should it be necessary.

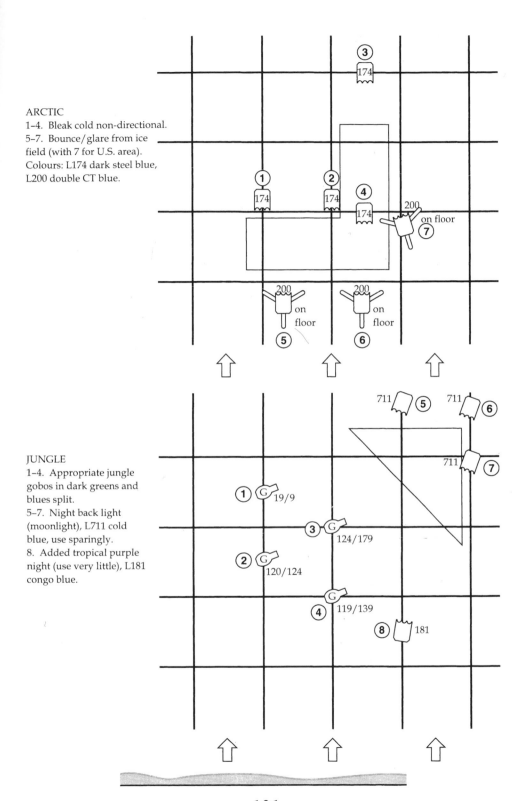

ARCTIC
1-4. Bleak cold non-directional.
5-7. Bounce/glare from ice
field (with 7 for U.S. area).
Colours: L174 dark steel blue,
L200 double CT blue.

JUNGLE
1-4. Appropriate jungle
gobos in dark greens and
blues split.
5-7. Night back light
(moonlight), L711 cold
blue, use sparingly.
8. Added tropical purple
night (use very little), L181
congo blue.

Analysis – Exercise 39

The awkward mark-out areas in this exercise are designed to make you create lighting that often requires more than one luminaire for any angle, and therefore continues to test your blending together of general cover.

The designs require a choice of luminaire, position, key source, and colour, and there are no perfect answers. However, the key source should be suggestive of the sun or moon and this underlying tenet should be unmistakable when looking at the finished piece.

The use of leaf gobos to suggest light through trees comes into its own in this type of exercise: although you do not have to use them, if used imaginatively and subtly they provide an easy and emotive way in which to evoke the natural world, especially where the set is giving you little support. Leaf gobos (alongside the more unspecific break-up gobo) are probably the most used in the catalogue.

Fig. 60 illustrates a few solutions of my own to these exercises.

The creation of a general cover therefore is about the blending together of acting areas on stage. It allows for continuity of angle across an area and as a consequence also gives the lighting designer control over smaller parts of the stage. The continuity of angle is particularly important for light that has high visibility to the audience, such as light on faces. Because of this, lighting designers often divide the stage into bigger areas for back or top light which cuts down on the amount of equipment used. On a big stage a general cover may be drawn as illustrated in Fig. 61.

A general cover that allows for a central area is often of greater use than one that does not as this is usually the dominant part of the stage and it is very practical to be able to lift, separate, and close down to the centre line.

It makes life easier for the lighting designer if the same units are used to light any given part of the general cover. Likewise it is easier if each area of the stage is divided up into chunks of the same size, but this does not always have to be the case. It may be that on a set with specifically dedicated areas it is more useful to design the general cover to accommodate these delineations (see Fig. 62).

The next exercise continues to expand on the concept of creating a realistic general cover.

EXERCISE 40
GENERAL COVER 6 – INTERIORS

In your chosen area create another general cover which will clearly suggest the interior of an office to the audience. It is important in this exercise to

A GENERAL COVER OF LIGHT

1. Conventional front cover in five sections across and two up/down stage.
2. Top light in L159, six areas (2K fresnels?).
3. Angled back light in L103.
4. One side light opposing back light angle (*see also* diagram page 114).

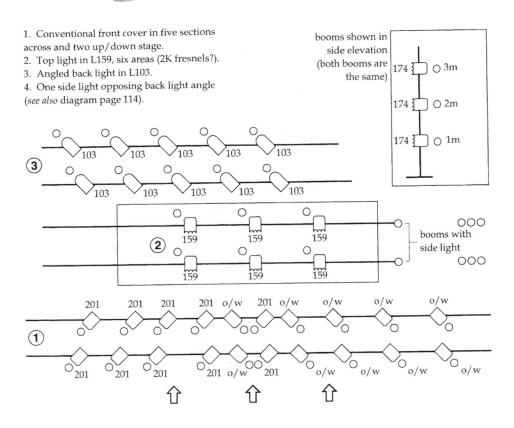

Fig. 61 *Solution to Exercise 39 (above).*

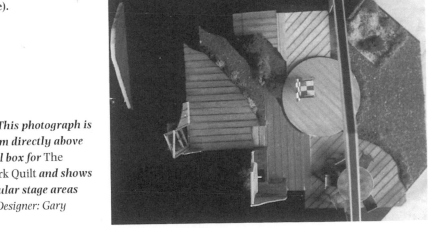

Fig. 62 *This photograph is taken from directly above the model box for* The Patchwork Quilt *and shows the irregular stage areas clearly.* Designer: Gary Thorne.

make sure the cover is fully comprehensive, that the corners and edges are lit exactly the same as the centre. Once again think three-dimensionally of objects within the space.

Analysis – Exercise 40

Once more there are many solutions to this exercise. Window gobos can be very useful as a shorthand means to communicate information about a specific interior location: the use of a venetian blind gobo would suggest the office setting perfectly. The placing of a single, bright and well-defined light source that interjects itself on to the stage may seem to go against the concept of a seamless, perfect general cover. In a way it does, but the idea is that the very clarity and familiarity of the image (in this case, the light through a window) leaves the audience in no doubt as to why this part of the stage is more brightly lit than any other. It also allows us to highlight any part of the stage we wish.

The creation, manipulation and subtle use of a general cover pervades many a stage production and a lighting designer needs to become proficient in its construction and use. The following exercises can be used to develop these skills. The exercises include many commonplace themes (time, place, season, and so on) although some are a little more bizarre (see also exercises in Chapter 12, page 152).

EXERCISE 41
ATMOSPHERES

a. Having chosen a performance area and an audience point of view, create one or more of the following lighting states (see list below). Change your designated theatre space as often as you need – either producing each exercise in isolation or as part of a bigger rig aimed at producing radically different moods for the same space.

b. As you become proficient give yourself difficult areas to use with odd shapes, or an area where height is restricted.

c. Limit your equipment, number of circuits, or time. Better still, get someone else to impose reasonable (or unreasonable) limitations on you.

d. Remember that you are lighting for performance as well as simply creating the right mood. Thus it is important that within each piece the lighting allows the actors to be sufficiently visible for a scene of some length. Visibility, along with homogeneity, is important over the whole stage area.

e. If you are unsure about how to proceed with these exercises look at the examples included in the exercise analysis below.

Create the Following:
a. Dawn in the city
b. The surface of the planet Mars

c. A school classroom on a warm, sunny day

d. A dark and dank cave

e. A luxurious Arabian palace

f. A hot day in the Australian outback

g. Inside a sauna

h. The surface of the moon

i. Christmas morning (around the christmas tree)

j. A desert island

k. A church interior

l. A hot and steamy nightclub

m. A bus shelter at night

n. A medieval castle

o. An igloo

p. A morgue

q. A cold Victorian library

r. Inside a beehive

s. Sunset on a moor

t. A hot, sunny picnic in a hay field

u. A bleak, rainy day at the seaside

v. A ballroom

w. Inside a ghostly mansion

x. A busy fairground at night

y. Inside a cathedral

z. Inside a vast, intelligent machine.

Analysis – Exercise 41

Some of my solutions to the exercises above are illustrated in Fig. 63.

The next exercise in this chapter takes the notion of the general cover and ties it in with our desires concerning the use of lighting angles.

EXERCISE 42
THE FIRST TEN
LUMINAIRES

This exercise is about looking at the stage as a single area and deciding how to light it with very limited equipment. It makes us review our thinking in terms of what we want from stage lighting. Use the stage area shown in Fig. 64 to carry out the following exercise:

a. Show how you would light the first stage area if you only had one luminaire and indicate what type of unit it would be. Remember that the luminaire will need a beam size sufficient for the job in hand.

b. With a second area use two luminaires. With each new area *all* lanterns can be relocated.

PLOTTING

In most of the practical exercises lighting states have to be plotted on to a lighting control. Here are a few tips:

1. Build states from a black-out, starting with the most important unit in your rig, such as the key light.
2. Put somebody on stage to light on to. This is called 'walking'.
3. Start with units at 40–60 per cent, leaving yourself somewhere to go.
4. Do not be afraid to start again if things are not working.
5. Set timings and run cues to test them.

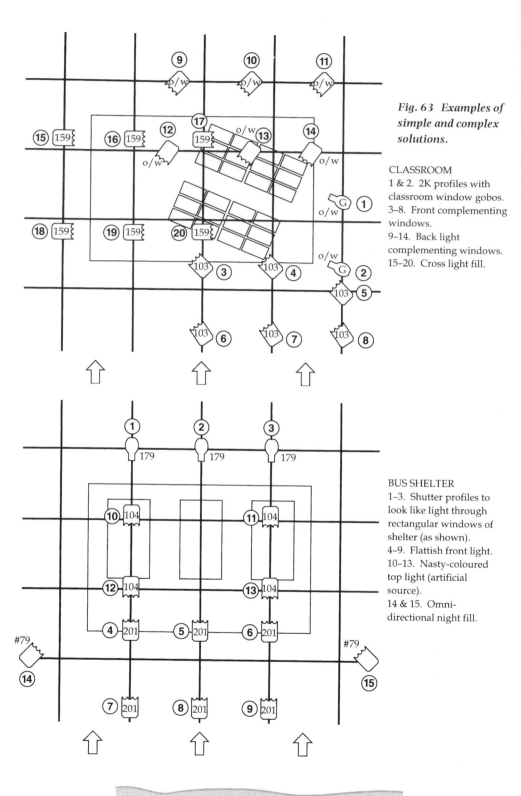

Fig. 63 Examples of simple and complex solutions.

CLASSROOM
1 & 2. 2K profiles with classroom window gobos.
3–8. Front complementing windows.
9–14. Back light complementing windows.
15–20. Cross light fill.

BUS SHELTER
1–3. Shutter profiles to look like light through rectangular windows of shelter (as shown).
4–9. Flattish front light.
10–13. Nasty-coloured top light (artificial source).
14 & 15. Omni-directional night fill.

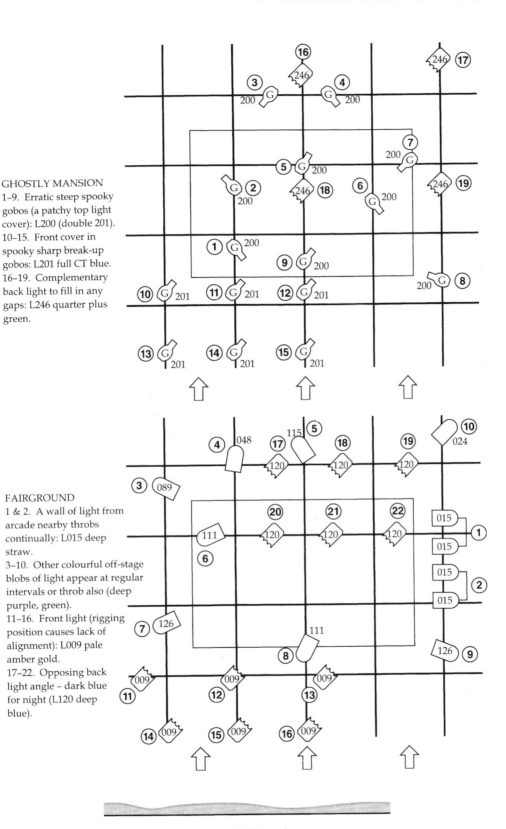

GHOSTLY MANSION

1–9. Erratic steep spooky gobos (a patchy top light cover): L200 (double 201).

10–15. Front cover in spooky sharp break-up gobos: L201 full CT blue.

16–19. Complementary back light to fill in any gaps: L246 quarter plus green.

FAIRGROUND

1 & 2. A wall of light from arcade nearby throbs continually: L015 deep straw.

3–10. Other colourful off-stage blobs of light appear at regular intervals or throb also (deep purple, green).

11–16. Front light (rigging position causes lack of alignment): L009 pale amber gold.

17–22. Opposing back light angle – dark blue for night (L120 deep blue).

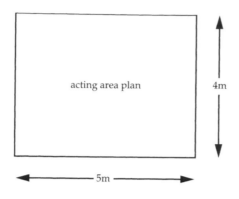

Fig. 64 An acting area plan, 5m (or yards) wide by 4m (or yards) deep (Exercise 42).

c. Light successive areas with an extra unit each time.

d. If you decide you have enough units to divide the area make sure you illustrate clearly the area each luminaire is covering.

Analysis – Exercise 42

This exercise is based in part on the chapter 'First Steps in Lighting Design' from Francis Reid's splendid publication *The Stage Lighting Handbook*. Reading this chapter will act as an analysis for this exercise and is central to the next.

EXERCISE 43
A CRITIQUE OF 'FIRST STEPS IN LIGHTING DESIGN'

Read the above chapter. Do you agree with use of the first ten luminaires?

Can you say why his choice varies from your own in Exercise 42?

Analysis – Exercise 43

Throughout the recent development of stage lighting, Francis Reid has been and still is the foremost commentator and a great inspiration. His lucid explanations of the technical and the creative have never been bettered. All of his books are worth reading but the seminal work *The Stage Lighting Handbook* remains the most readable of introductions to stage lighting, and his *Lighting the Stage* the most reassuring.

With this in mind it is instructive to look at this important chapter with a view to what we have been discovering for ourselves. I have opinions that differ from those of Francis Reid and I expect you will disagree with us both on some points.

It is important to note that what Francis Reid is doing in this chapter is, of course, different from the intention given in Exercise 42 above. He is using his example to promote ideas already discussed in his text. Thus the following critique is valuable to us but perhaps a little unfair to him. His solutions are part of an initial look at lighting the stage whereas mine attempt a more sophisticated approach based on our discoveries up to this point.

Luminaire 1 – Fig. 65

The first luminaire has to address visibility and FR places his out front centre.

A GENERAL COVER OF LIGHT

Fig. 65 General cover with 1 unit.

My solution does the same but allows us just a little sophistication in directionality. It is also clear that FR wants this unit to be a fresnel in order to cope with the size of cover being asked of it, which makes good sense.

Luminaire 2 – Fig. 66
The second unit allows for a more comprehensive coverage of actors in the space, and I find no difficulty in agreeing with FR here.

Luminaire 3 – Fig. 67
The third unit sees FR adding some characterful back light and doing so from an interesting angle. Again I have no problem with this but wonder why at this point the illustration shows it as a profile

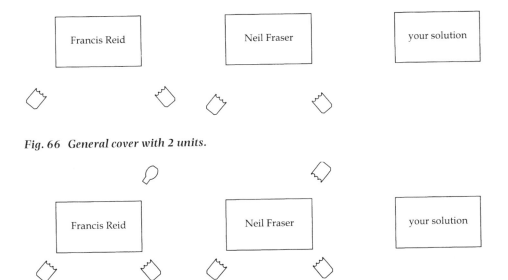

Fig. 66 General cover with 2 units.

Fig. 67 General cover with 3 units.

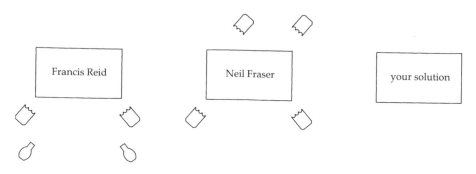

Fig. 68 *General cover with 4 units.*

when it will still need to be covering quite a large area and probably from even closer than the front light.

Luminaire 4 – Fig. 68
Using four pieces of equipment FR abandons his back light and allows himself greater control of the stage by splitting it into two areas, up- and down-stage. The desire to gain area control may be strong but losing the back light is a shame. Using so few units means that the lighting is going to be sparse whatever we do. Also at this point it becomes clear that FR is thinking of a space of such size that he needs a profile for the front-of-house positions in order to project light over distance to the stage. This traditional use of units is perhaps rather misleading in such an abstract exercise. In my version we stick with our back light and retain a sense of key by directing from one side only.

Luminaire 5 – Fig. 69
With his fifth unit FR brings back the back light. With my fifth unit I thin my back light but divide the stage as he did previously and thus we arrive at much the same point.

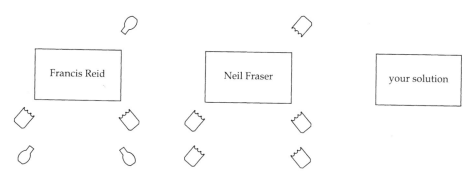

Fig. 69 *General cover with 5 units.*

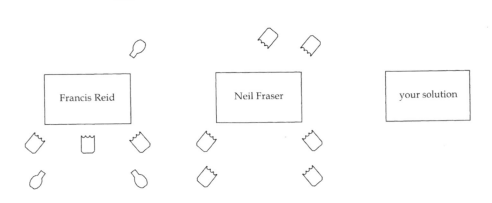

Fig. 70 *General cover with 6 units.*

Luminaire 6 – Fig. 70

This unit really confuses me. FR suggests that his two units up-stage may create a hole centre-stage that needs filling. Providing we are using good-sized units there is no reason why this should be so and his fill light washes over the other more interesting angles. My sixth unit adds to our rather thin back light instead.

Luminaire 7 – Fig. 71

Adding this unit FR finds himself with enough equipment to divide the up-stage area in two. Whilst the up-stage area further from the audience is the right one to choose, the down-stage area is now covered a little thinly on the

FILL LIGHTING

A 'fill' light is a unit rigged to add to the stage picture in such a way as to counteract hard angles, for example, to fill in the face if only steep front angles are in use. It is perhaps better to call them alternative angles rather than use the weak-sounding term 'fill'.

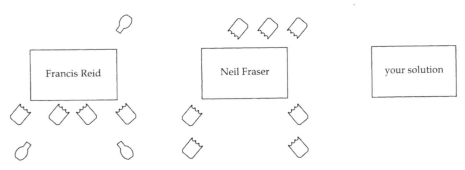

Fig. 71 *General cover with 7 units.*

SPARES

A lighting designer may choose to add units to a rig in positions, such as the centre of a bar, which may be of use in unforeseen circumstances. This may save time later or be considered a waste of time initially. Also it does tie the lighting designer into using certain positions whatever the problem.

front and complementary angled back light. We could have built up the front light to arrive at this point throughout, but perhaps only now can we afford to risk such one-sided directionality because we know the back light will clearly support it. Also we can now use smaller beamed units and so perhaps profiles are at last in order.

Luminaire 9 – Fig. 73
FR's ninth unit allows him a more sophisticated division of the down-stage area. Mine allows for a basic back-up opposing the main angle of front light.

ground. My seventh unit continues to add to the back light which is still over-powered by the front.

Luminaire 10 – Fig. 74
For his final unit FR adds to his back light. I feel that whereas his final solution allows for stage divisions it leaves creative dimensionality rather thin on the ground still. My tenth unit adds to the cover. In fact the next two units would allow me to finish the job completely (*see* Fig. 75).

Luminaire 8 – Fig. 72
FR is still lighting rather flatly and adds a down-stage front light fill at this point. My solution sees a radical change of heart. We now have enough equipment to divide the stage into four areas each with an angled

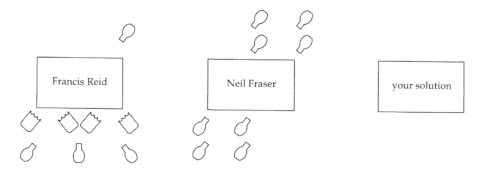

Francis Reid   Neil Fraser   your solution

Fig. 72 General cover with 8 units.

A GENERAL COVER OF LIGHT

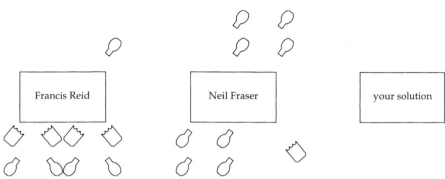

Fig. 73   General cover with 9 units.

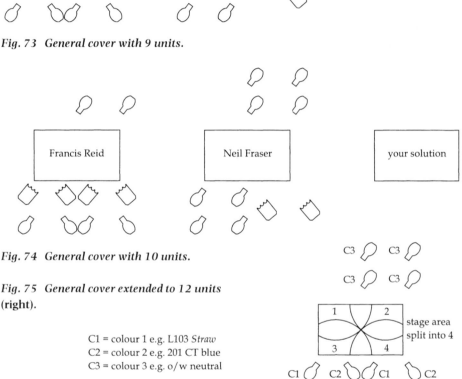

Fig. 74   General cover with 10 units.

Fig. 75   General cover extended to 12 units
(right).

C1 = colour 1 e.g. L103 *Straw*
C2 = colour 2 e.g. 201 CT blue
C3 = colour 3 e.g. o/w neutral

Summary

By the end of this chapter it should be apparent that our understanding of stage lighting has become quite profound. We can consider and exe-cute pieces of work as diverse as the light on a desert island or the atmos-phere of a Christmas morning. By con-sidering the concept of general cover we have faced the more technical side of decision making as well. General cover is, of course, only part of a lighting design which may also incorporate

COLOUR WASHES

A basic covering of the whole stage (or large area), using a few large units, usually to add a telling colour.

any number of specials, colour washes, isolated areas, and effects. A production may also necessitate more than one general cover or a general cover that can be used in a number of guises (*see* Fig. 76).

To become better lighting designers we now need to practise our craft as much as possible. This we will continue to do, whilst ever expanding our knowledge of equipment and techniques, in the next chapter.

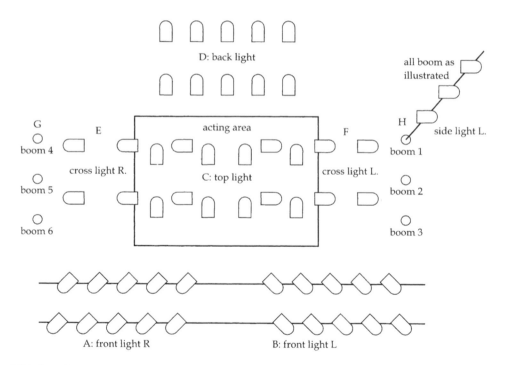

GENERAL COVER: OPTIONS (*see* also Fig. 61 page 103)
Note: stage covered from 8 distinct angles A–H; if all used at once the stage would be overlit (i.e. no shadows).
Good cover options: A + F, A + F + G, B + D, B + D + G, G + H, G + H + D, and so on.
Note: each angle would be in its own colour, and all units from each angle would have the same colour.

Fig. 76 A complex general cover.

9

Movement in Light - Lighting Effects and Intelligent Luminaires

'We Are the Movers and Shakers'

Light in Motion

This chapter deals with the notion of adding movement to our lighting. All of the exercises so far have had solutions that suggest a static (single-state) piece of lighting. However, by changing or moving the light we add a whole new dimension to our work, and a greater potential to evoke imaginative responses from the audience. Light can be said to 'move' by changing in direction, intensity, colour, or shape. The final part of this chapter discusses the most modern of lighting instruments, the so-called 'intelligent luminaire' – a moving light unit that has the potential to change all these things at our command. But even without this exciting technology, the basic equipment we have already used can be made to move light most effectively. In the next exer-cise we start to play with this idea of light in motion.

EXERCISE 44
THE ELEMENTS

Create a piece of lighting in an area of your choosing (not too big) to suggest the theme of the four elements: earth, water, air, fire.

Analysis – Exercise 44

This exercise can be addressed in a number of ways. The elements may be represented symbolically or naturalis-tically. The latter in particular would necessitate the use of lighting cues to modulate or move the light. Gobos may well be of use, and for water and fire some sense of their motion being illus-trated in the finished lighting would be most beneficial. Careful manipulation

CUES AND TIMINGS

A normal fade from one state to another is described as a cross fade. More sophisticated controls allow for cues to start at different times and run at different speeds. These are called move fades.

Most modern controls allow cues to operate at set timings ranging from one second to twenty minutes. In the case of recordable timings the cue can be split so that units fading in run separately from units fading out. These split timings allow for cues to overlap and mould together.

of cues – fading from one unit to another to suggest movement – can work very well. However, there are a number of special lighting effects available which put real motion into light and can be of great use.

MOTION EFFECTS

These can be divided into two main groups:

1. *Animation Effects.* (a) The animation wheel. A pierced wheel that fixes on to the front of a luminaire and rotates at a fixed or variable speed. It is generally used on a profile unit in conjunction with a gobo and can be used to suggest fire, water, wind, rain, trees in motion, a passing train,

and so on (Fig. 78). (*Note:* The first, simple, fixed-speed animation discs were called KK wheels.) (b) The gobo rotator, which does as its name suggests, can also be fixed or variable speed and is similar to an animation wheel, but produces a less real effect.

2. *Effects Projectors (EP).* These are special luminaires that are used in conjunction with effects wheels – in this case a painted glass disc that rotates in front of the effects projector at a

Fig. 77 Cloud projection.

Tangential Breakup

Radial Breakup

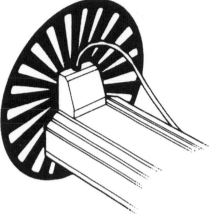

Fig. 78 DHA animation disks. All offer alternative motion effects, for example, water ripple.

Spiral Breakup

Linear Breakup

Triangle Breakup

Cloud Breakup

Elliptical Breakup

Dot Breakup

Flicker wheel

Coarse Radial Breakup

Coarse Tangential Breakup

Colour Wheel

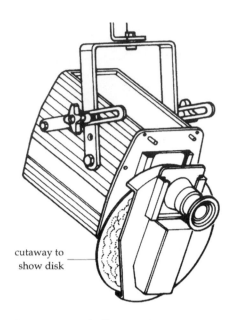

cutaway to
show disk

Fig. 79 Typical effects projector.
Fig. 80 A UV scene **(below).**

fixed or variable speed, and depicts a more graphically 'real' effect of fire, water, rain, moving clouds, and so on (Figs 77 & 79).

If you are lucky enough to have access to some of these lighting effects try the next exercise.

EXERCISE 45
USING LIGHTING EFFECTS 1

Repeat the previous exercise using motion effects where you think appropriate.

Analysis – Exercise 45

See Fig. 82 for my answer to this exercise. I have suggested enhancing the lighting

OTHER LIGHTING EFFECTS

1. Tubular Ripple: produces the effect of rippling light - very good on bottom of cloth to suggest light on distant wave tops.
2. Fuzz Light: rotating warning light - red, blue, green, orange.
3. Scanners and Helicopters: disco effect rotating narrow beam spots.
4. Strobes: for wild, slow-motion effect, or single flashes. Strobes in tubing - Arcline, Flexiflash.
5. Ropelights: conventional lamps in tubing - cabled to chase along their length, giving the effect of movement.
6. Mirror Balls: for that ballroom effect or more imaginative use. Can be of various shapes other than spherical.
7. Fibre Optics: woven into cloth or set - cat's eyes and starcloths.
8. UV (Ultra Violet) or Black Light: used for transformation effects in combination with luminous costume or make-up (*see* Fig. 80).

(*See also* Colour Changers, page 66.)

Fig. 81 Special effects devices.

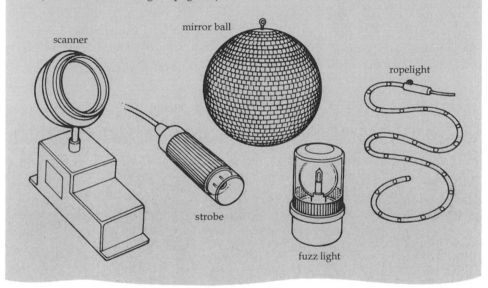

scanner
mirror ball
ropelight
strobe
fuzz light

by the provision of a smoke or dry ice machine. A modern, subtle, mist effect can be very effectively achieved by using a 'cracked oil' smoke machine (*see* Figs 84 & 85). Using smoke or a mist to show the light beams (as in a mist) is a common practice in all forms of theatre, especially dance, where the set is often very minimal. They can of course also be used to suggest real smoke.

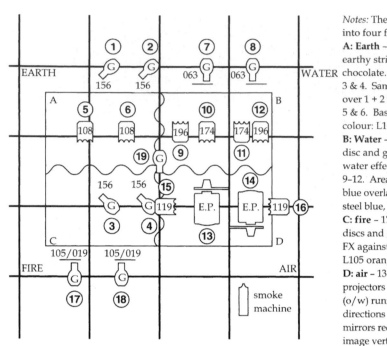

Fig. 82 The four elements (Exercise 45).

Notes: The area has been split into four for clarity.

A: Earth – 1 & 2. Gobos of earthy stripes: colour: L156 chocolate.

3 & 4. Same gobos but crossing over 1 + 2 to give hatching effect. 5 & 6. Basic background colour: L108 english rose.

B: Water – 7 & 8. Animation disc and gobos for reflected water effect: L063 pale blue. 9–12. Area split into four watery blue overlapping areas: 174 dark steel blue, 196 true blue.

C: fire – 17 & 18. Animation discs and gobos for fire flicker FX against a dark unlit floor: L105 orange, L019 fire.

D: air – 13 & 14. Effects projectors with fleecy cloud FX (o/w) running in opposing directions (N.B. diverting mirrors required to project image vertically). 15 & 16. Dark blue sky colour for back-drop in L119 dark blue.

Fig. 83 Typical smoke machine (note fluid container).

Fig. 84 Smoke and gobos used to suggest Olde London Town for Scraps. *Contact Theatre Co.*

EXERCISE 46
USING LIGHTING EFFECTS 2

Using whatever equipment you have at your disposal and in a small area of your choosing, create one or more of the following:

a. An underwater scene.
b. A ski lodge with a raging fire just off-stage.
c. The flight deck of a space ship.
d. The inside of a magic castle.

Analysis – Exercise 46

These exercises require a good understanding of the best effects to use:

SMOKE AND DRY ICE MACHINES

B e careful when using smoke and dry ice machines on stage – very specific rules and regulations must be applied. The substances used can be very dangerous: smoke can cause breathing problems if over-used, as can dry ice which can also burn.

Seek professional advice before using.

a. An animation wheel, or a projected water ripple are both suitable.
b. An animation wheel would be best.

DHA LTD

Founded by a top lighting designer, David Hersey Associates is the main UK manufacturer of gobos and animation effects.

c. & d. Almost anything would do. It is how you use the effects that is really important. Subtle and clever use of effects can mean that even the simplest equipment can make magic (*see* Fig. 85).

It may well be that you are already conversant with effects equipment and

Fig. 85 A simple gobo splits the light into beams – caught in smoke.

have been using them in exercises prior to this chapter. If not, from now on they should become part of your repertoire, as they are for any lighting designer.

The next exercise continues to expand their use.

EXERCISE 47
USING LIGHTING EFFECTS 3

(Uses text from Weapons of Happiness *by Howard Brenton)*

Create some lighting for the London Planetarium scene in Howard Brenton's play *Weapons of Happiness*. This scene contains two people seated on stage as if part of the audience watching the display. Use as many effects as you have available as well as conventional units to show the reflection of the display on the actors.

1. Light on actors – dim.
2. Back light actors – dim.
3 & 4. The sun bright:
L015 deep straw.
5. Flexiflash unit runs across stage ceiling for comet.
6. Pluto: L181 congo blue.
7. Neptune: water FX split colour: 196 true blue, 200 double CT blue.
8. Uranus: L241 fluorescent.
9. Saturn: gobo rotators doing ringed circles: L121 green, L131 marine blue.
10. Jupiter: big wash L237 CID to tungsten, L238 CSI to tungsten.
11. Mars: L106 primary red.
12. Sunrise from boom: L151 gold tint, L152 pale gold, L153 pale salmon.
13. Extra B/L for sunrise L103 straw.

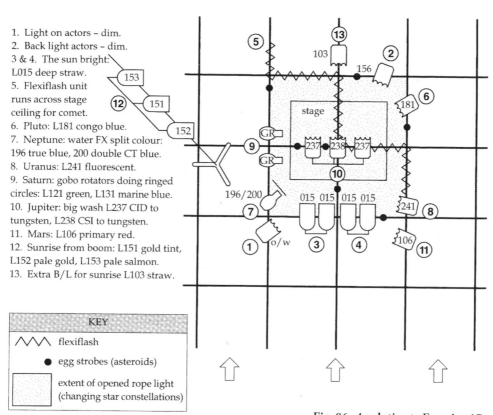

KEY	
/\/\/\	flexiflash
●	egg strobes (asteroids)
▢	extent of opened rope light (changing star constellations)

Fig. 86 A solution to Exercise 47.

Analysis – Exercise 47

Fig. 86 shows a suggestion for this rather complex piece. On a real stage it may also be possible to enhance the scene with a few more literal effects. On my plan I have used a series of connected small strobes (a flexiflash) to suggest the comet, and rope lights to suggest changing constellations – all of which is to be suspended above the action. A back cloth or projection screen, available as a piece of scenery, would open up other such opportunities (*see* Chapter 10).

INTELLIGENT LIGHTING

Luminaires that can re-point themselves; re-focus; change size, shape and colour; add and subtract gobos, shutters and irises are described as 'intelligent', although obedient would be more accurate! Intelligent luminaires are all based on the remote control of motor-driven parts and there are two main types.

1. The whole unit moves (examples include *VL5*, *VL6*, and *Martin 600*).

Fig. 87 Vari* Lite's 'VL6' (above). Strand's
'Pirouette' with scroller (below)

2. A mirror moves to deflect the beam
   (for example, *Goldenscan*).

Manufacturers such as Vari*Lite and
Martin make units that are like profiles,
fresnels, and parcans but with all the
additional features mentioned above.
Other manufacturers make simpler, usually fresnel or par-based units, such as
Strand Lighting's *Pirouette* which re-
angle but do not change size, shape, or
gobo, and only change colour if a scroller
is added to the front (*see* Fig. 87).

If you are lucky enough to have
access to such an instrument here are
some exercises to get you going.

EXERCISE 48
MOVING LIGHTS 1 –
FAMILIARIZATION –
TARGET PRACTICE

a. Place six objects of varying sizes in
   your theatre space.
b. Place the equipment so that it can
   be programmed to light any of the
   objects.
c. Plot a sequence of cues based on pick-
   ing options out of the following five
   lists (*see* chart opposite) at random:

Analysis – Exercise 48
A lot will depend here on what equipment you have. However, the essential
thing is to develop an ability to plot the
many parameters available quickly and
accurately. (Race each other to see who
can plot the quickest.)

List 1 OBJECT	List 2 SIZE	List 3 INTENSITY	List 4 COLOUR	List 5 SPEED OF MOVEMENT
1	Largest beam	@ 50 per cent	Blue	10 seconds
2	Smallest beam	@ Full	Green	30 seconds
3	Tight to object	@ 20 per cent	White	1 second
4	Gobo in	@ 45 per cent	Yellow	0 seconds
5	½ object only	@ 60 per cent	Red	7 seconds
6	Next to the object	@ 70 per cent	Orange	20 seconds

Having mastered the equipment let us now look to its creative use.

EXERCISE 49
MOVING LIGHTS 2 – CREATIVE USAGE

Use your intelligent lighting to create a new piece of lighting for any of the exercises indicated below, or try the new one:

a. Exercise 44 – The Elements
b. Exercise 58 – Fireworks
c. Exercise 60 – The Cyc' 2 – By George!
d. Exercise 74 – Plotting Practice – *Son et Lumière*

NEW EXERCISE
'BEAM ME UP SCOTTY'

In an area of your choice create the following:

a. A piece of lighting to suggest the bridge of a starship. Either work from your imagination, or watch a TV programme or film.
b. Create a second lighting state for 'red alert'
c. Use effects to create the effect of 'beaming up'.

The actor will be brought into position by scenic devices, appearing as if by magic (this is not your problem – the lighting is!)

Analysis – Exercise 49
Getting the lighting right for the bridge and red alert effects should not pose too much of a problem as it is just another atmospheric general cover with the need for a feeling of futuristic, hi-tech equipment. The beaming effect is not so easy – even the best effects equipment in the world cannot match the possibilities available on film.

The use of intelligent lighting on stage is still in its infancy. Although already producing amazingly beautiful effects on musical stages across the world, its more

Fig. 88 This photo from Polka Theatre's production of The Starlight Cloak *gives some idea of the potential for stage magic – in this case the projection of gobos and woven lights in the actor's costume allow him to become one with the night sky.*

subtle creative use in the full range of theatre genres is still to be explored.

SUMMARY

Moving light of any kind on stage is a powerful tool and one we should eagerly add to the range of options before us. As with any strength it can be used rather bluntly and the watchword when using these devices should always be *subtlety*. Even the humble gobo has been so abused in the past that many directors refuse to have them in their productions: this is a great shame given the beautiful and subtle use that they can be put to. It is up to the lighting designer to encourage the director to accept the full range of possibilities in light by judicious use of the equipment, especially the effects.

We are now more fully equipped to work on the exercises of dramatic mood and atmosphere that we will examine in the next chapter.

10

MOOD AND ATMOSPHERE

'Is this a Dagger I See Before Me?'

Fig. 89 *The tough life on the streets from* Arturo Ui. *Contact Theatre Co.*

I n the Introduction to this book I noted that 'Good stage lighting adds character to space, texture to object, emotion to event, impetus to action, and powerful dramatic emphasis to a stage picture'. We now understand how this may be achieved through our choice of lighting angle, the way we shape and colour the light, and whether we use a lot or a little of any single source. Each luminaire is like the key on a piano, used in a multitude of different combinations to create the visual equivalent of music. We know how to draw attention to action by illuminating it. We can place a performer in both realistic and dramatic contexts, and can charge and then change the emotional atmosphere of the drama at any moment.

Much of our attention so far has been devoted to the creation of realistic scenarios, although even here we have acknowledged that there is much scope for artistic interpretation. In this chapter the exercises become more abstract and we will need to exploit fully our artistic and technical resources.

EXERCISE 50
CONTRASTS

Part 1

a. Choose two small areas within the theatre space, and mark them out with tape on the floor.
b. Establish the audience point of view – perhaps mark it with a taped arrow on the floor.
c. Put a rig up to light the two spaces to represent and/or illustrate the abstract concepts of hot and cold (one in each area) as follows:

  1. In each area try to create a visual representation of the theme involving as many aspects of the theme as you can.
  2. The end result may naturally involve a series of cues rather than a static state.
  3. You may place anything you wish in the areas, but do not spend too much time on this as the lighting is more important. The object is only there to allow the different angles and colour of your light to be more fully seen, so any three-dimensional object would do.

Part 2

Repeat the exercise with any of the following pairs:

a. Big and small
b. Black and white
c. Thick and thin
d. Hard and soft
e. Love and hate.

Analysis – Exercise 50

This exercise starts us thinking in terms of the abstract. A lighting designer often has to interpret the mood of a dramatic piece, understand the underlying tensions and emotions of a dramatic event or dialogue, and then translate this mood onto the stage. In doing so the lighting designer is working with a wide range of abstract themes and emotions.

The exercise makes us think about our perceptions of and reactions to quite everyday concepts but then asks us to describe them using light. Through the use of opposite pairs, our ideas will be polarized and clarified by the need to contrast one theme with the other.

As is often the case, there are no right or wrong answers to the exercise. However, it can be extremely valuable to seek the opinion of someone that does not know what the themes are, as this will tell us whether we have kept faith with the general perceptual concepts of an audience and translated the themes well. The themes have been specifically chosen for ease of interpretation and should not be left until you are happy with your work on them.

The next exercise seeks to take the concept of abstract interpretation of ideas or themes further.

MOOD AND ATMOSPHERE

Notes:
HOT = one soft focused
orangy outside – inside red
pool of light..
COLD = sharp blue angular
gobo pattern..

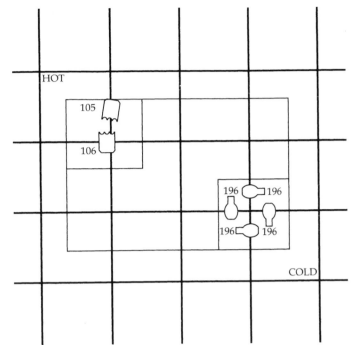

*Fig. 90 Suggested
solution to Exercise 50
(right). Four solutions to
exercise variations,
showing appearances of
lighting rather than rigs
(below).*

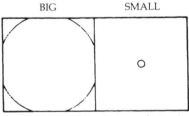

Note: uses 2 profiles (big uses shutters)

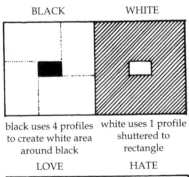

black uses 4 profiles   white uses 1 profile
to create white area   shuttered to
around black   rectangle

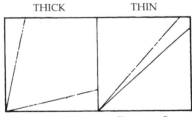

beams of light horizontally across floor:
fresnels with differing size of focus

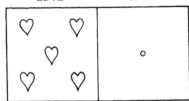

gobos in pink?   small dot in green
(profiles)

EXERCISE 51
OPPOSITES

a. Choose a small area in your theatre space and light it to suggest one of the following pairs of opposites. You may place an object or objects in the space for the light to be seen upon. Be sure to remember the audience point of view.

    1. Good and evil
    2. Nice and nasty
    3. War and peace
    4. Love and hate
    5. Fact and fantasy.

b. Repeat the exercise as many times as you find useful.
c. If you only undertake one or a few of the pairings listed above, take a little time to think through how you would have tackled the others, particularly how they would have differed from each other.

Analysis – Exercise 51

The themes in this exercise concentrate the mind further on how to express feelings with light – how to tune into an emotional mood and interpret it with shape, colour, and direction of light. The way the units are used in combination with each other should also become increasingly sophisticated.

As a general rule in these exercises 'less is more' often applies, a simplicity or purity of thought deriving from a clear usage of lighting techniques can often be most effective. As with the previous exercise, an independent point of view and interpretation of your finished product would be invaluable.

The themes in this exercise also call upon the lighting designer to make decisions about the intensity of effect. For example, the difference between the depiction of good and evil as opposed to nice and nasty. Such degrees of attenuation, the subtleties between emotions similar to each other, lead us to fine-tune our responses to the dramatic stimuli (*see* Fig. 51).

The next exercise takes a single theme that may be developed further than the paired themes. However, there are some restrictions on the equipment as would be likely in a full production.

EXERCISE 52
MAGIC

a. Create a piece of lighting within a small area of your theatre space to describe magic.
b. Remember to establish an audience point of view.
c. You may use only six luminaires.
d. You may use any colours, gobos, or other effects that are available.
e. Repeat the same exercise with any of the following topics:

    1. Mystery   2. Celebration
    3. Fantasy   4. Horror
    5. Music.

Fig. 91 Suggested solution to Exercise 51.

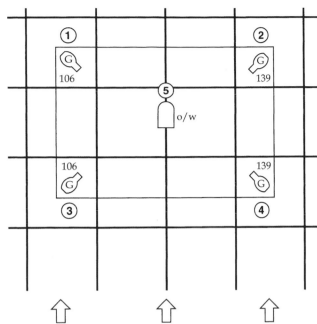

WAR AND PEACE

Notes: lighting pile of upturned chairs placed centrally (could be two separate piles).

1 & 4. Flash opposite to:

2 & 3 = war in violent colours.

5. Appears powerfully and still = peace: L106 primary red, L139 primary green

Fig. 92 Suggested solution to Exercise 52.

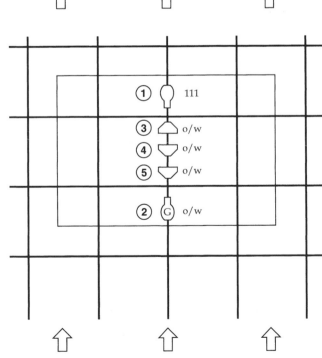

MAGIC

Notes: focus on floor.

1. Creates a box to surround:

2. Any appropriate magic symbol: gobo = rabbit?

3–5. Three floods flash on and wash out the image, when they die away 2 has gone!

Analysis – Exercise 52

This exercise seeks again to develop the imaginative use of light to depict mood. The themes allow for a broad response. A decision must be made as to whether to use the cliché to communicate or avoid it and thus risk becoming too obscure. One of my solutions is illustrated in Fig. 92.

The next exercise takes a similar line but reminds us that often the mood is derived from a character in a context rather than just the context itself.

EXERCISE 53 CHARACTERIZATION IN LIGHT

a. Imagine an actor standing or seated in your theatre space, with you, the audience, facing him or her.

Fig. 93 Lighting for character: Lolita Chakrabarti as Minnehaha in Hiawatha. *Torch Theatre.*

b. Create a piece of lighting to provide a dramatic context for the actor as described in one or a number of the following moods:

1. Heroic
2. Demonic
3. Angry
4. Frightened
5. Sad
6. Joyful
7. Bored.

c. This exercise will work best if you can get somebody to stand or sit for you when focusing and plotting the lighting.

Analysis – Exercise 53

You should have found from this exercise that is possible to give an actor a dramatic context to support the mood of the piece. The extent to which you succeed in doing this will depend on the degree of subtlety and nuance that you put into the finished work.

Your lighting of the actor should now show a greater sophistication than would have been demonstrated in the very similar requirement in Chapter 5 (Exercise 16). Is this the case, or has the simplicity of those early responses become cluttered and messy? A lighting designer must always be able to get back to basics: once again the general rule that 'less is more' must be borne in mind.

The next exercise is once again more abstract. It deals with the need to find convincing lighting solutions in an apparent vacuum of ideas by using your inner imaginative resources.

Fig. 94 *The steep angle of light combines with the costume to show a heroic, faceless hero from World War One in* Oh! What a Lovely War. *Contact Theatre Co.*

EXERCISE 54
STUDIO/STUDIO

Create an exciting, innovative and inspirational piece of lighting within your theatre space – create an *environment* – as follows:

a. The whole volume of the space must be used, and although not every surface needs to be lit, the whole space must be incorporated into the finished piece. The theatre space is the environment.
b. There must be enough light for the audience to walk around within the space without bumping into each other.
c. You may only use eight pieces of lighting equipment.
d. If available (and desired) a smoke machine may be used (*see* page 119).
e. One scenic element may be used to add to the space if you feel it would be useful, but it should not dominate – the theatre space itself remains the environment.

Analysis – Exercise 54

This exercise has any number of solutions. The lighting designer must create an environment from very little external input – unlike the other exercises no theme is given here. This is not unusual in the theatre world and it is good to know that you have the inner resources to make 'something from nothing'.

In contrast, the next exercise comes with a plethora of external references. It delves further and deeper into the realm of abstract interpretation of ideas, and for the first time makes use of a text.

EXERCISE 55
BLACK BOX

Black Box

The star is falling so it prove a stone.
Flight Zero, moon, is flashing
us goodbye.

———————————

Because we could not bear to be alone
We talk our deaths down nightly
from the sky.

———————————

In darkness, in the Dreamtime,
we have flown
Over the mountain where our
picked bones lie.

Kit Wright

a. Create a piece of lighting to accompany the reading (on tape, or from off-stage) of the poem above.
b. It is required that you light on to a suitable object such as a screen. Remember to establish an audience point of view.
c. The director has commented that the theme of the piece is darkness, 'the small light of consciousness in the vastness of life's loneliness'. He has said that 'Above all the quality of

darkness is as important as that of light'.
d. You may choose the area to light, and place the set as you see fit.

Analysis – Exercise 55

Using a poem as a text upon which to base a piece of lighting saves us the trouble of having to read and understand a whole play. But with a poem such as Kit Wright's the complexity makes it every bit as deep. Throughout our work in theatre there is an almost constant need to interpret ideas; whether they are coming from the director, designer, actors or the playwright. Text analysis, therefore, is an important part of this work.

In this poem we have obvious visual references to latch on to and interpret or reproduce naturalistically. Having gathered these references we need to decide what the poem is saying and thus how we should place these visual ideas if we choose to use them.

There is obviously an aircraft image at work here: 'black box', 'flight zero', 'we have flown over the mountain', but also a deeper meaning about our lives. Perhaps the sun is the falling star and in the long term it is falling towards us to final destruction, that is why the moon is 'flashing us goodbye'. And because we feel alone in this knowledge we greet our deaths 'talked down nightly from the sky' and have become familiar with them by flying 'over the mountain where our picked bones lie'.

We are thus all victims of the inevitable plane crash of existence.

If this is to be our interpretation, we would light the piece accordingly with any visual references attuned to this doom-laden scenario and what the director has already told us. Loneliness becomes the essence of the mood we wish to create. Obviously we are not alone in finding our interpretation – the director and designer, amongst others, are there for us to turn to if we feel that we need help. Figure 95 shows a rig derived from my earlier interpretation of this poem.

Note: For other chances to work with a cyclorama *see* Exercises 58, 59 and 60 in the next chapter.

Any poem may be of use for such an exercise, but short poems with some concrete visual references are particularly useful. Listed in the information box below are a few which have been used very successfully by my students.

OTHER SUITABLE POEMS

The Truly Great by Stephen Spender
Vision and Prayer by Dylan Thomas
Letter in November by Sylvia Plath
Exits by Kit Wright
Alone in the Woods by Stevie Smith
The Trees by Philip Larkin
Rainforest by Judith Wright
Prelude 1 by T S Eliot
Midsummer, Tobago by Derek Walcott

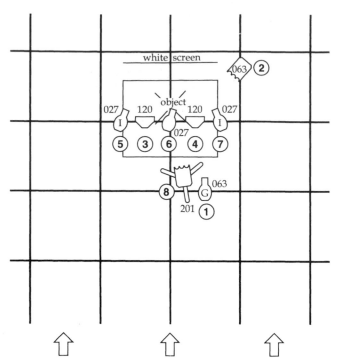

Fig. 95 Suggested solution to Exercise 55.

BLACK BOX
1. A glass moon gobo hovers faintly in the:
3 & 4. Night sky.
2. Moonlight is cast across our object.
5-7. Three very small red dots twinkle in the sky randomly.
8. Our object lit from below casts a shadow like a mountain range onto the sky – it fades away.
I = iris.
Colours: L063 pale blue, L120 deep blue, L027 medium red, L201 full CT blue.

SUMMARY

Working from a number of different starting points we have begun to really stretch our imaginative resources. In doing so we have also tested to the full our knowledge of lighting instruments and our understanding of the lighting design conventions and techniques discussed earlier in this book. We have needed all these resources to realize fully our creative imaginings.

At this point it can be said that we are truly working as lighting designers, reacting to influences and suggestions, interpreting ideas and moods, allocating equipment to suit the need, and creating appropriate and exciting landscapes of light.

However, in this chapter it has been necessary on occasion to give ourselves objects to light. Creative exercises have required a scenic element rather than a person on which to cast our light. This is an area into which we should delve further. The next chapter looks in more depth at lighting the set.

11

LIGHTING THE SCENERY

'All the World's a Stage'

In any staged production the performers mainly provide the drama. With our lighting we have been providing these actors with a context. Perhaps the chief provider of context is the scenery, the 'set', which also needs to be lit for maximum impact.

A set can often provide a good canvas on which to display times of day, changing seasons, or any dramatic shift of atmosphere, especially if it is a

Fig. 96 Set model. The Starlight Cloak. *Designer: Gary Thorne. Polka Theatre Company.*

Fig. 97 Detail of texture. Beowulf. *Designer Gary Thorne. Polka Theatre Company.*

Fig. 98 Set model. A Patchwork Quilt. *Designer Gary Thorne. Polka Theatre Company.*

THE SET MODEL

The set designer will often produce a scale model of the set. The lighting designer should take every opportunity to view it both for ideas on how to treat it, and also to spot any potential problems where a piece of set may cause restrictions on where to place the lighting equipment or on the light beams crossing the stage. If possible borrow the model and shine light on to it, trying colours, shapes and angles across it.

non-moving edifice of some size, as it is easier to see the lighting on static scenery than on smaller, moving actors. This applies also to a stage floor, especially if the audience is made very aware of it by their situation, for example, an audience in raked seating looking through the action at the stage floor.

Because we know that a painted wall cannot in itself change, we realize that if it does change in appearance this is the effect of the light. Thus the scenery allows us to communicate to the audience what the light is doing.

The set designer is usually given a greater prominence in the production team than the lighting designer. This is because, along with the director, he or she originates the production style of the piece (*see* page 152). Historically this has also been the case, mainly because until recent times stage lighting has remained relatively inflexible, whereas the art of the scenic painter developed a degree of sophistication very early in the history of staging. It is a mistake to think that stage lighting was not complex until the advent of electricity (*see* box overleaf).

Many of the previous exercises have concentrated on the lighting of objects. A stage set is just another object to which we must apply our knowledge about the way that light works.

The following exercises allow for more practice in this and also look at some of the more specific scenic elements that we may have to deal with.

EXERCISE 56
'HONEY, I SHRUNK THE SET'

a. Create a set in miniature on a table-top or similar, using everyday objects to represent the walls and other objects on the set. You may use anything that comes to hand, but things you have in quantity will be particularly useful (paperback books, children's building blocks, cereal packets, toilet roll tubes, matchboxes, beer bottles).

b. Make a decision about your stage floor and create this accordingly, using either a coloured piece of paper, fabric, or other material.

c. Create your set to represent one of the following settings (it may be abstract, realistic or anything in between):

    1. A cityscape
    2. A battlefield

A BRIEF HISTORY OF LIGHTING IN THE THEATRE

The Ancient World
Sunlight, torches, candles, oil.

The Age of Shakespeare
Mostly sunlight, candles.

Italian Renaissance
Mobile candlelight, polished bowl reflectors, coloured liquids as lenses, and silks also to colour, basic dimming by covering the oil lamps with hoods, footlights in use by c.1628.

English Restoration
Candles with reflectors, footlights.

The Eighteenth Century
Oil lamps, primitive control.
1765 David Garrick at Drury Lane copies the French theatre by removing unconcealed lights above stage that shone in the eyes of the audience.

The Nineteenth Century
1803 The Lyceum theatre is first to use any gaslight, and by 1817 becomes totally gas lit.
1843 Haymarket is last theatre in London to convert to gas.
1826 Limelight invented. An oxygen and hydrogen mix burning on a block of lime. First really bright light source in a directional unit. Usually used for spotlighting the actor.
1838 Henry Irving introduces the darkening of the auditorium, and control of all light from the prompt corner.
1846 Electricity as a light source is first used in the Paris Opéra to spotlight the actor.
1863 Charles Albert Fechter sinks footlights below stage level.
1878 Incandescent electric bulb used in Paris Hippodrome.
1879 California theatre in San Francisco becomes first US theatre to be lit by electric light.
1881 Savoy in London opens with electric light – 1,158 lamps are used.
1886 Paris Opéra fully converted to electricity.

The Twentieth Century
A number of theatre practitioners theorized about lighting, notably Adolphe Appia, Edward Gordon Craig, Mariano Fortuny, and Josef Svoboda. The century ends with fully automated computer controls and luminaires.

Other names to look up: Sebastiano Serlio, Leoni di Somi, Angelo Ingeneri, Josef Furttenbach, Nicola Sabbattini, Henry Angelo, Philip de Loutherbourg, Hubert von Herkomer.

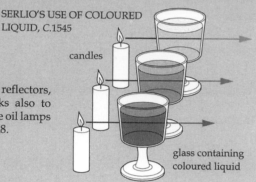

SERLIO'S USE OF COLOURED LIQUID, C.1545

candles

glass containing coloured liquid

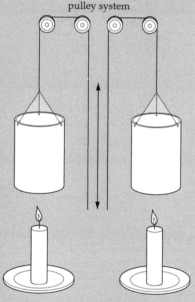

SABBATTINI'S DIMMING MECHANISM, 1589

pulley system

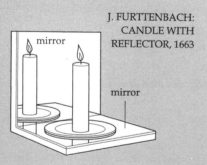

J. FURTTENBACH: CANDLE WITH REFLECTOR, 1663

mirror

mirror

Fig. 99 Historical lighting techniques.

FIRE PRECAUTIONS

Be careful that what you choose to make your model with does not prove to be flammable under the heat of the lighting.

Always keep a fire extinguisher to hand in your theatre space and make sure you know how to use it.

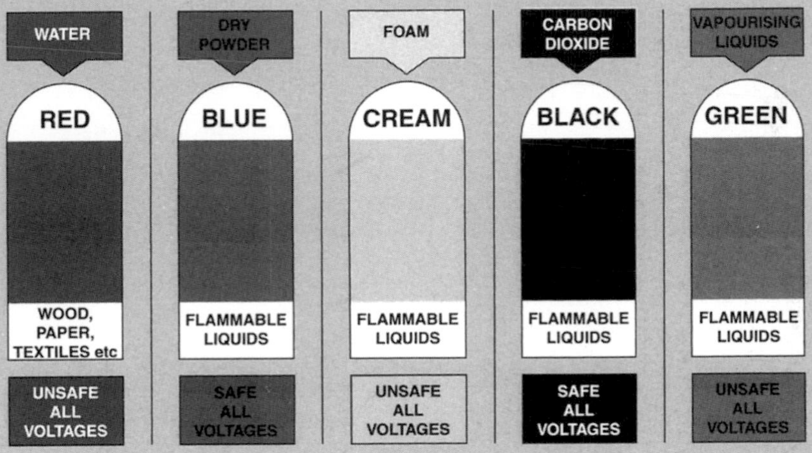

WATER	DRY POWDER	FOAM	CARBON DIOXIDE	VAPOURISING LIQUIDS
RED	BLUE	CREAM	BLACK	GREEN
WOOD, PAPER, TEXTILES etc	FLAMMABLE LIQUIDS	FLAMMABLE LIQUIDS	FLAMMABLE LIQUIDS	FLAMMABLE LIQUIDS
UNSAFE ALL VOLTAGES	SAFE ALL VOLTAGES	UNSAFE ALL VOLTAGES	SAFE ALL VOLTAGES	UNSAFE ALL VOLTAGES

Fig. 100 Fire extinguishers, with coding for different types.

3. A dungeon
4. A palace courtyard
5. A forest.

d. Light the whole stage with your equipment to best show off your set, and to create any of the following moods:

1. A bleak morning
2. A hot summer day
3. Night-time with moonlight
4. Tragedy
5. Comedy.

Analysis – Exercise 56

There is no end to the solutions and variations inherent in this exercise, and it may be one you want to try a number of times.

By creating the set in miniature you can more easily make impressive visual statements with a single unit, such as a wash of colour, or gobos. On a larger scale such statements would require more equipment, but still be possible. With the use of shutters and irises smaller parts of the set can also be isolated and given special treatment.

CYC'S AND GAUZES

The back wall of a stage space is known as a cyclorama – or cyc'. It is usually white and can be either a fixed wall or a cloth *(see* Cyc' Floods, page 48).

A gauze is a cloth that can be transparent or opaque depending on the lighting *(see* Exercise 61).

Many of the aspects of lighting we have already covered will be used again in this exercise including the use of thin, oblique angles to enhance and exaggerate texture on the set; gobos to add texture to otherwise flat areas; the use of back light to silhouette and thus display shape; the use of strong colour to make emotional connections; and so on.

The next exercise suggests variations to take your understanding further.

Fig. 101 An all-white setting: Jaqui Gunn's set for The Tempest. *Contact Theatre Co.*

EXERCISE 57
EBONY AND IVORY
(BLACK AND WHITE SETS)

a. Repeat Exercise 56 choosing the settings and moods at random, but this time with:

    1. An all-white set
    2. An all-black set.

Note: A quick way to get total white or black would be to put a cloth or sheet over your objects.

Analysis – Exercise 57

Lighting designers often shy away from sets that are all-white or all-black, but there is no reason to do so. They present a striking visual context to an audience and are therefore quite popular with set designers. The trick is to make use of what they offer, and if necessary explain to the director what the limitations may be.

Your experimentation should reveal the following (*see* Figs 101 & 102):

All-white sets are great for showing colour and shape to the audience – it is

Fig. 102 All-black sets do not show off colour or shape and need more light, but they are great for isolation and mysterious, dark moods – making it possible to float the performers in an undefined space. The Tempest. Contact Theatre Co.

like lighting a large, three-dimensional projection screen. Any light source will glow on such a set and less light is needed to create effects. This also provides the main limitation which is that with such a propensity for bounce it becomes more difficult to isolate individuals or areas without illuminating things you do not want to see.

The use of a back cloth or projection screen behind or as part of our stage setting opens up further lighting possibilities. We need to know how to use scenic elements such as cyc's, cloths and gauzes. The following exercises are designed to help you to gain this knowledge.

EXERCISE 58
FIREWORKS

Hang a white sheet or screen to act as a back cloth, with a small acting area in front of it. Treat this as your night sky and light it for a short firework display incorporating the following:

a. A number of fireworks explode into colourful sparks in the sky (create one, two or three).
b. The glow of a nearby fire can be seen on the faces of actors standing on stage.
c. Some low fireworks explode off-stage and this is also seen in the faces on stage.
d. Put a moon in the sky, and moon-light on the stage.

e. Put clouds in the sky.

Analysis – Exercise 58
Simply creating the night sky can be quite a challenge in this exercise. A cyc' is an unusual and often unique element on stage – costumes and scenery usually occupy a darker, more varied range of colours. Colours appear to react more vividly on the white, flat field of a cyc' than on other stage elements. You will find that quite strong colours are required to register on the cyc' as so much white is available to bounce back (*see* Colour notes on page 66). When putting the clouds into

PYROTECHNICS

Real stage fireworks are often also the province of the lighting department. They come in several guises:

1. Maroons – that go bang.
2. Gerbs – that sparkle like roman candles.
3. Smoke-creating devices.
4. Confetti or streamer-throwers.

SAFETY NOTE

Stage fireworks are one of the most dangerous stage devices – *do not* use them without specialist training or advice.

the sky you have the choice of static elements like gobos, moving effects wheels, or projectors.

Figure 103 illustrates my solution to this exercise.

One major problem with the cyc' is keeping unwanted light away from it. If the acting area is very close to the cyc' then cross-lighting the action is one solution. Otherwise the careful blending in and colouring of light on the bottom of the cyc' becomes imperative.

The lighting of a cyc' features in the next exercise (*see also* Exercise 55).

EXERCISE 59
THE CYC' 1 – HEAVENS ABOVE

Using just a cyc' or projection screen create:

a. A bright, realistic daytime sky with clouds

b. A sky at sunset.

Analysis – Exercise 59

Getting an even cover of light on a cyclorama is best achieved with cyclorama floods. If either of these are not

FIREWORKS
1. A dark night sky: #79 bright blue.
2 & 3. A firework flashes on 2 and changes colour 3 (gobos).
4 & 5. Other fireworks explode in the sky and change colour rapidly, sparkling and dying away (gobos and colour wheels).
6–8. Other ground fireworks are lit, flicker and fade away nearby.
9 & 10. There are pale night clouds in the sky.
11. A moon (iris) and:
12. Moonlight (back light).
13. Off stage a fire flickers.
14–16. General cover.

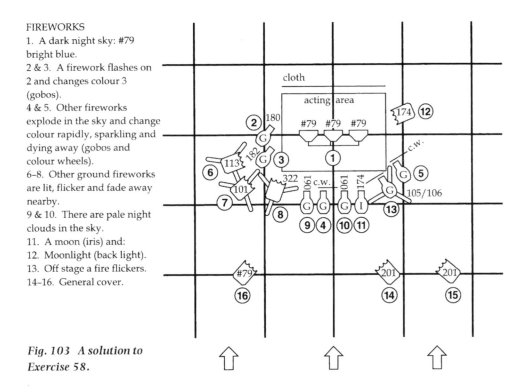

Fig. 103 A solution to Exercise 58.

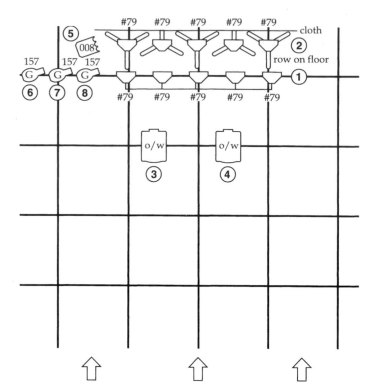

Fig. 104 A solution to Exercise 59.

HEAVENS ABOVE
1. Sky in bright blue (#79); floods are often paired thus (a good use of bigger dimmers i.e. 5k).
2. Ground row of floods prevents cyclorama tailing away at bottom.
3 & 4. Cloud FX projectors.
5. Sunsets S.R. warm glow from sun out of sight: L008 dark salmon.
6–8. New striated clouds appear replacing the bigger moving FX with elongated flat strips across the horizon: L157 pink.

available or you are in a studio with a low ceiling or grid, other units may have to be used.

Again a depth of colour is required. Interestingly a cyc' can be lit for both day and night with the same colour. This is because context is everything: try, for example, using Rosco 79 with a daytime and night-time stage created in front of it.

Moving cloud effects are very pretty but can often become annoying, especially if set to move across the 'sky' rather quickly. Sometimes static clouds are preferable, especially for the sunset when colour is perhaps more important than movement.

Figure 104 illustrates my solution to this exercise.

EXERCISE 60
THE CYC' 2 – BY GEORGE!

Using just a cyc' or projection screen creates a piece of lighting to support a presentation of *Sunday in the Park with George* by Stephen Sondheim. Use a cast recording – play it into your space – and use only the short section of the opening sequence up to the word 'harmony'.

Fig. 105 Visual interpretation. The opening sequence of Sunday in the Park with George.

Analysis – Exercise 60

This is a short piece but it provides a number of stimulating challenges. The piece itself is an aural description of an artist's understanding of the use of paint to create the real world around him and he is particularly aware of the role of light in this. The lighting designer has the problem of translating this into real light. The best way to achieve this is to take the abstract ideas and interpret them into discordant shapes, images and colours that finally fall into place – into 'harmony'. Of course there will be any number of solutions to this, Fig. 105 shows my thoughts on this exercise.

EXERCISE 61
GAUZES

Hang a scenic gauze (or an old net curtain will do) to cut across your acting area, then carry out the following:

a. *Hamlet*, Act III, Sc. IV. Create lighting for the Closet Scene with a candle-lit feeling and incorporating Polonius behind your gauze. It is important that Polonius is seen at some times and not at others. Also, project an appropriate heraldic gobo on to the gauze.
b. Experiment with different gauzes if you have them.

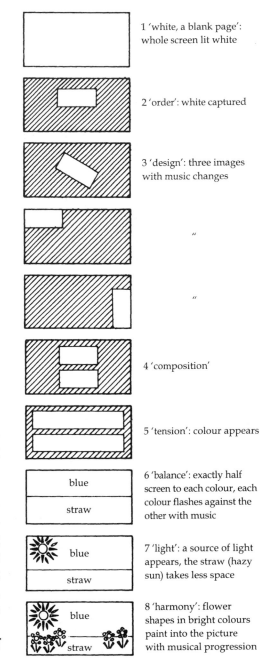

1 'white, a blank page': whole screen lit white

2 'order': white captured

3 'design': three images with music changes

"

"

4 'composition'

5 'tension': colour appears

6 'balance': exactly half screen to each colour, each colour flashes against the other with music

blue

straw

7 'light': a source of light appears, the straw (hazy sun) takes less space

blue

straw

8 'harmony': flower shapes in bright colours paint into the picture with musical progression

blue

straw

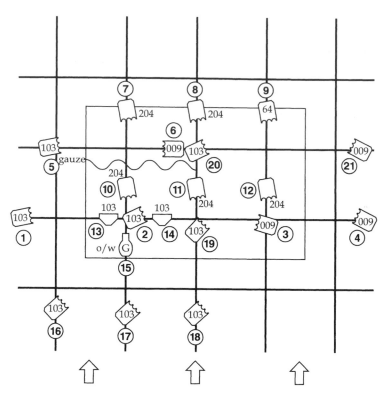

Fig. 106

HAMLET ACT III,
SCENE IV
1 & 2. Steeply angled
front/cross light (keeping
off gauze) from S.R.
3 & 4. From S.L.
5 & 6. Same cover behind
gauze.
20 & 21. Same cover
beside gauze.
8–12. Back/top light rest
of stage.
13 & 14. Fill light on front
of gauze.
15. Heraldic gobo on
gauze (needs to be flat-on
so image is not distorted).
16–19. Front light rest of
stage, that is D.S.
N.B. this plan attempts to
light the behind gauze area
to match the rest of stage –
this may not really be
necessary: 7 alone may
suffice.
Colours: o/w – straw range.

c. If you are unsure about using the gauze, read the exercise analysis below before proceeding.

Analysis – Exercise 61

The basic rule with gauzes is that when lit from the front with no light behind them they are solid looking, but when a scene is lit behind them with no light in front they appear transparent. Obviously, it is sometimes difficult to keep all the light off the gauze when you want to, or to keep all the area behind it unlit when required. This is not necessarily a big problem but it will weaken the effect you are trying to achieve.

With some types of gauze, light is allowed through and the scene lit behind when you do not want to see it. This is sometimes a problem when using a gobo as you may wish to project it straight onto the cloth to get the best rendering of a symbol. An oblique angle of light hitting the gauze will do less damage in this way.

In a more realistic setting a lighting designer must think of ways to introduce convincing light-sources – the following exercise makes this point.

EXERCISE 62
SPOT THE LIGHT –
PLACING PRACTICALS

Think of places in Fig. 107 where practical light sources may be incorporated into the set and pencil them in.

Analysis – Exercise 62

Not all the practical fittings you could use here may be needed; the set may become cluttered with all of them – a conversation with director and designer may be of use here. Go into such a conversation knowing what equipment you would find most useful and guide them accordingly.

It is useful on a realistic stage-setting to maintain a balance across the space – even if you only need a practical stage-right, another light source stage-left will allow you to give a visual balance to the scene.

It is a very good idea to research an idea or theme relevant to a production. The following exercise encourages such techniques. The examples I have used are those I have found most commonly developed into a production style.

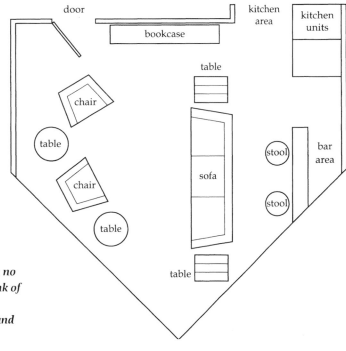

Fig. 107 Plan of set with no
light fittings shown. Think of
pendant fittings, table
clamps, standard lamps and
integral fittings.

Fig. 108 'Practical fittings' – in this case small strip lights – are being used to squeeze light behind the cut-out set pieces where a conventional luminaire would not fit. This has the same effect as back lighting the object – making it stand out from the background, and giving depth to an otherwise flat piece of scenery. Tonight at 8:30. *Kennington Studio, RADA.*

EXERCISE 63
RESEARCH – PERIODS AND STYLES

Research one of the following art movements or practitioners. Produce notes or sketches relevant to the subject. Create a piece of lighting inspired by or intending to represent the subject.

a. Film Noir
b. Art Deco
c. Expressionism
d. Surrealism
e. The work of Georg Grosz
f. The work of Hogarth
g. The work of Picasso.

Analysis – Exercise 63

In some cases the lighting of these themes becomes almost scenic and can greatly add to the stage setting. Here are a few notes of how I have approached some of these concepts:

a. Film Noir: black and white tones; dark shadows; strident angles and shapes; Venetian-blind gobos; ceiling fans; cigarette glows; matches being struck in darkness (*see* Fig. 109).
b. Art Deco: use of warm, sepia tones; multi-lined shaping of light; fans of light; high, diagonal angles.
c. Expressionism: strange weird shapes and colours; disjointed uneven lines across faces; stark, steep angles.
d. Surrealism: non-contextual use of obvious imagery such as literal gobos out of context; weirdly moving shapes.

SUMMARY

This chapter should illustrate the need to remember to incorporate the set into your thinking when planning the lighting design. Some equipment at least should be dedicated to 'dressing' the set rather than the action.

Play texts, rather than scenic pieces, are the real impetus of theatre work. The themes in Exercise 63 are already leading us in this direction. The next chapter allows us to apply our wide range of skills to the needs of a script.

Fig. 109 Brecht's Arturo Ui *set in thirties USA, lit as a Hollywood film noir thriller.*

12

WORKING FROM THE TEXT

'The Play's the Thing'

The starting point for most theatre productions is the printed word: the production style as conceived by the director/designer derives from this, as does the process of creating the lighting design.

In some productions the text (including stage directions and scenic descriptions) may be only a starting point for ideas, in others it is strictly adhered to at all times: productions differ greatly from one another in this respect.

Alongside the production style the text can be thought of as the single most important piece of research material for the lighting designer, and it is very important to know how to read a text and make good use of it in developing the lighting. This chapter explores the relationship between the word and the vision.

Our abstract exercises have been good practice for the time when we have to work according to the director's production concept. The next exercise involves the creation of a visual mood from the reading of a text.

EXERCISE 64
THE CAUCASIAN CHALK CIRCLE

a. Read *The Caucasian Chalk Circle* by Bertolt Brecht.
b. On a bare stage create a piece of lighting for the 'Chalk Circle' scene (scene six). Make the lighting appropriate in atmosphere for the setting itself and the drama of this part of the play.
c. The director also has the following requirements:

   1. Specials for the main characters (the two mothers and the judge) to define their emotional and dramatic role within the scene.
   2. The need to create the chalk circle in light – the drawing of it by the actors to thus be symbolic rather than actual.
   3. To make sure the lighting has a 'Brechtian' feel to it.

d. You may choose the area to light, and place and move the actors as you see fit within your theatre space. Remember to establish your audience point of view.

Analysis – Exercise 64

Although this exercise is based on a real play, it may be approached in much the same way as the other more abstract exercises in this chapter.

The lighting designer has to make decisions based on reading the text and interpreting the mood and atmosphere. So, for example, you may choose a strong, bright, cold top light (L200) to define both the circle and the general chilling arena surrounding it, making this the main feature of the piece and eschewing a specifically naturalistic key light for a more interrogatory, courtroom-like source. As in previous exercises, light is used here to define characters specifically. Equipment also needs to be chosen to delineate the chalk circle.

The lighting designer also has to take the notes given by the director and act upon them:

a. Specials are required to define the emotional position of characters in the scene. This demands the same understanding of the link between light and character that we have already been experimenting with.
b. The need to create the chalk circle in light demands a choice of luminaire or luminaires to create the circle, and also a decision about how

the light getting to the stage floor to do this job will affect the actors it may pass through.
c. To make sure the lighting has a 'Brechtian' feel to it demands a bit more from us. Researching a theme, a historic period, a dramatic style or, as in this case, a theatre theorist and practitioner is quite a common feature of a lighting designer's work. Directors and designers often refer to such as a means of describing the production style or mood of lighting they are looking for.

DESCRIPTIVE TERMS FOR LIGHTING

Terms used by directors and designers to describe lighting often include reference to artists and works of art. For example, 'I want the lighting to have a "Rembrandt", or "Caravaggio", or "Dutch Master" look'. This would often involve side light and other such characterful angles (*see* Fig. 134).

Other terms include:
Chiaroscuro (shadowy interplay between light and dark).
Brechtian (stark, white and bright).
Impressionist (colourful, gentle, subtle).
Expressionistic (rough, sharp, brutal, gaudy).

For this exercise we need to understand a little (or a lot) about the dramatist

WORKING FROM THE TEXT

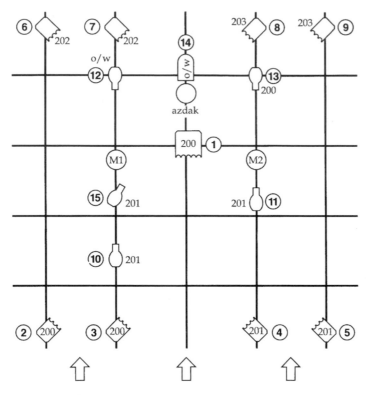

Fig. 110 Suggested solution to Exercise 64.

CAUCASIAN CHALK CIRCLE
1. Strong fresnel in wide focus defines circle (i.e. 2K or 5K unit).
2–9. Front and back light cover – symmetrical to support circle/arena concept.
10 & 11. Specials on two mothers (M1+M2), one steeper and thus nastier than the other – colours to suit also.
12 & 13. Back light on mothers.
14 & 15. Specials on azdak: the judge strong top but warm.
Colours: all in range open white – double CT blue (i.e. cold-austere).

BERTOLT BRECHT 1898–1956

Born in Augsberg, Bavaria. Dramatic expounder of Marxism. Exiled from Nazi Germany in 1933. Settled in California in 1941. Left US after appearing before the House Committee on Un-American Activities in 1947. Settled in Switzerland. Returned to East Germany in 1949, founded Berliner Ensemble with whom he worked until his death. His theories denounce Aristotelian dramatic emotion for a didactic, political drama using many abstract devices - puppets, banners, captions, music. Suggested the use of 'surprise' tactics to make the audience think rather than becoming emotional. For 'Alienation Technique' *see* Bibliography.

Bertolt Brecht and thus the term 'Brechtian' which derives from Brecht's work as a dramatist, director and theorist, in particular whilst with the Berliner Ensemble in East Germany after the Second World War (*see* above).

The term is applied to all manner of productions of this *genre*, not just his own plays.

In lighting terms, Brechtian is usually used to mean lighting that is stark, uncolourful (often with no gel), and strident. The need to create what we know as 'alienation' can also affect the way a lighting designer places and uses cues. The lighting becomes one of the devices used to make the audience aware that what they are watching is an artificial concoction, and that the production is asking to be thought about intellectually rather than just experienced – using stark lighting cues that jolt or surprise make for such moments of alienation.

This particular play, based as it is on the notion of a circle, opens itself to a solution based on an audience placed 'in-the-round' which will need the appropriate lighting.

Whilst continuing with the theme of using texts, the next exercise takes time out to look at the variations of possible staging, including in-the-round, and how the lighting designer needs to address them.

EXERCISE 65
THE MARAT SADE

In the previous exercise you may have put your audience all around the stage. In-the-round staging is not uncommon but requires some special consideration when being lit, as does any 'alternative' staging arena. If you have already attempted an in-the-round rig you may wish to read the analysis of this exercise straight away. If not, try the following exercise first:

a. Read the play *The Marat Sade* by Peter Weiss.
b. Place a performance area within the theatre space, with the audience on all sides.
c. Create a piece of lighting to suggest the bath-house of the asylum where the play within the play takes place, giving a suitably claustrophobic and hysterically intense atmosphere.
d. Place a number of specials within the scene for the following static locations:

   1. A place where the Maquis de Sade can sit and direct from.
   2. A central position for Marat in the bath.
   3. An area for a small part of the audience to be played to.

Analysis – Exercise 65

Lighting in-the-round is not as complicated as it may at first seem. The principles that govern the decision-making concerning the lighting remain the same as for any other piece of work. As usual, we have to make sure that a balance is struck between visibility and atmosphere, but we must do so from a greater number of viewpoints (*see also* Fig. 114).

Fig. 111 Photograph from a production of The Marat Sade *showing Marat and Charlotte Corday.* University Theatre. Manchester Drama Department.

It is wrong to think that it is imperative to give all the audience the same lighting picture. If this is achieved it usually means that the lighting is overly bright and rather boring. It is better to concentrate on giving all viewpoints a decent picture whilst accepting that it will be different for each member of the audience. For example, in a particular scene it may be that the action is heavily three-quarter back lit from one point of view, whilst from the opposite side of the audience a very strong, front-angled, key light is in evidence. The balance could then be swapped over for the following scene.

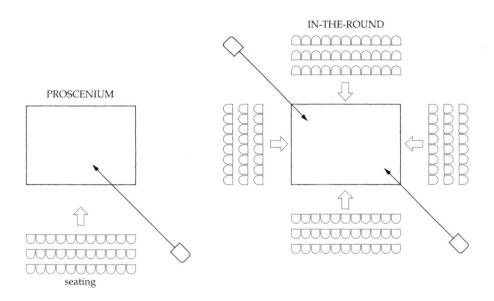

Fig. 112 Minimum requirement lighting angles. Although not ideal, consider how the actor would look from each seating block.

Some other things are also true of lighting in-the-round:

1. Top light gives a strong silhouette to the stage picture and *is* viewed the same from all around.
2. The audience is often close to the stage and more likely to be blinded by back light that is angled to act as someone else's front light – thus steep angles and the predominance of top light again applies.
3. The minimum lighting angles required to light an actor for visibility in proscenium is one, and for in-the-round is two (*see* Fig. 112). In the former case this is seldom satisfactory for a general state because it affords no 'shaping' light. Two angles, however, can be quite atmospheric in-the-round.

Other stage shapes are variations on the difference between the two extremes of straight proscenium staging and in-the-round. Similar problems occur in all cases and the lighting designer must take care to always think of the different audience viewpoints within one arena, even in proscenium (Fig. 113).

The next exercise offers a full text to work from.

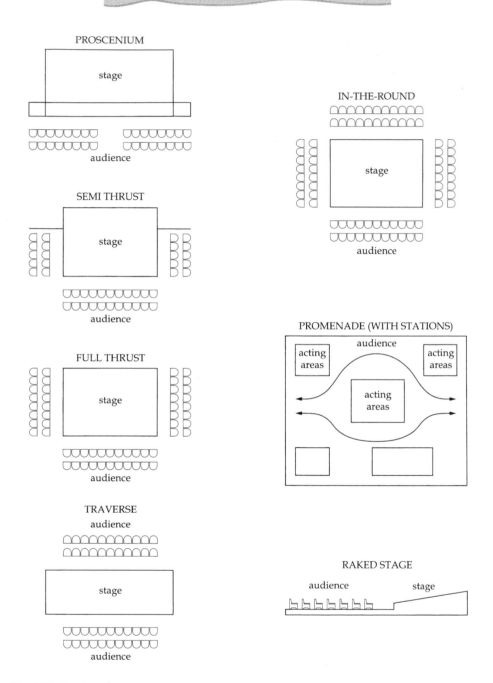

Fig. 113 *Staging shapes.*

Fig. 114 We must consider the audience's viewpoint in elevation, that is, the audience eye line (**right**).

Fig. 115 A solution to Exercise 65.

MARAT SADE
1–7. Intense dramatic ghoulish top light.
8–19. Front cover (think of it from each view point a–d) with 8–11 in light break-up gobo (i.e. softly focused).
20 & 21. Specials on Sade.
22 & 23. Specials on Marat (plus 7).
24 & 25. Audience area.
Colours:
201 full CT blue;
202 half CT blue;
246 quarter plus green;
242 Lee fluorescent 4300K;
241 Lee fluorescent 5700K.

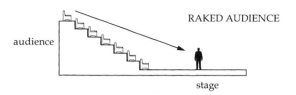

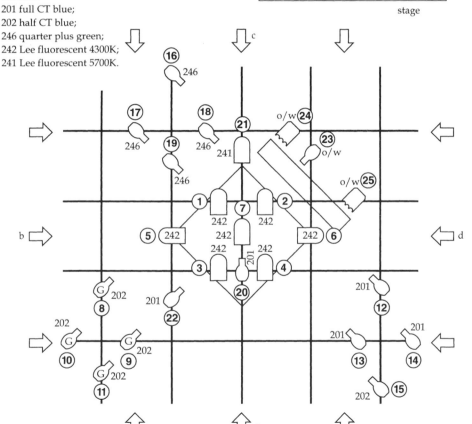

EXERCISE 66
AGAMEMNON

a. Read the Ancient Greek play *Agamemnon* by Aeschylus.
b. Create a short piece of lighting that:

1. Tells the story of the play.
2. Reveals the epic nature of the story.
3. Contains distinct visual references to the main characters from the play.

Fig. 116 A solution to Exercise 66.

Analysis – Exercise 66

There is no single solution to this exercise. However the mood of the drama suggests that the imagery used in the lighting should be bold and stark. The lighting also needs to suggest things like the 'ranking' of the characters (who is superior to whom), and individual characteristics such as anger, jealousy, or arrogance.

For example, if a single unit in a particular colour and shape is used to suggest a character; does the shape, colour, position or intensity of the light change

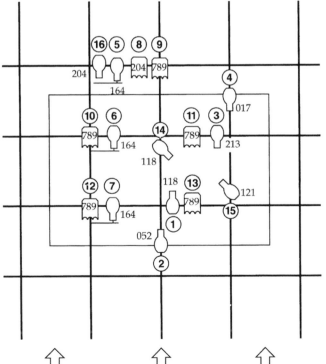

AGAMEMNON
Notes: characters are represented by vertical beams of light.
1. Agamemnon.
2. Cassandra.
3. Clytemnestra.
4. Aegisthus.
The heralds home is a warm beam (8) and door open look from unit 16. The message of Ag's return arrives in a series of localized fire flickers.
(7 to 6 to 5) Ag arrives to meet Clytemnestra etc. Ag moves nearer and greets him (14 & 15). Doorway goes red (9) then the stage is diffused in blood at Ag's death 10–13. 1 fades out.
Colours:
789 blood red;
052 light lavender;
118 light blue;
121 lee green;
213 white flame green;
017 surprise peach;
204 full C.T. orange;
164 flame red.

GREEK TEXTS

Ancient Greek plays are a useful source for lighting exercises as they are short, the stories are simple, and contain strong images. Examples include:

Oedipus Rex by Sophocles
The Bacchae and Electra by Euripides

Fig. 117 Oedipus Rex.

as the character moves through the play? When a character dies does the light die away also, or change in colour, or simply dim? Should the same rules apply to each character?

The characters need to be put into a dramatic context as well as individually identified. We need to know how they relate to each other, and in what kind of world they exist. In creating the world of the ancient Greek heroes and anti-heroes perhaps some strange elements could be included such as an unusual colour (green top light?) to suggest the very foreign nature of these strangely powerful antique plays.

Next, a longer and more complex play for us to capture in light.

EXERCISE 67
A SHORTER *WINTER'S TALE*

Read *The Winter's Tale* by William Shakespeare. Create a series of cues to represent the passage of time and emotional development within the play. The lighting cues are as follows:

a. The rich, happy court of King Leontes.
b. Sadness falling upon the court.
c. Time passes and the court decays.
d. The place of the statue.
e. The statue comes to life.
f. The court is rich and joyful once more.

Analysis – Exercise 67

Not all lighting cues are big scene-changing shifts. Indeed this exercise can be seen as being about shifting emotions. A number of the scenes display a need for cues within the lighting state. Bold images are required, but subtle nuances of mood are also needed, with cues internal to the scene that shift attention to a person or object, or allow for a subtle shift of atmosphere.

We often talk of cues 'closing-down' to or 'opening-up' from an individual on stage. Closing-down emphasizes an actor who at that point is the focus of attention, for a solilo-

TIMING OF CUES

The timing of a cue is dependent on the dramatic need of the moment. It should be totally in keeping with the flow of the play at that point. Fast cues are very dramatic and draw attention to themselves. Slow cues can be so slow as to pass unnoticed. The most common timing for a cue is between five and ten seconds. Cues are rarely longer than thirty seconds, although anything is possible. It often depends on how much time you have - a sunset could last for a whole scene – twenty minutes perhaps.

(*See also* box on Timings and Pre-Heats, page 165.)

quy for example. Opening-out makes the audience look at the 'bigger picture' once again. Closing-down cues would often require the isolation of a piece of stage using specials or a selected piece of general cover. The timing of such cues may be slow so that the actor seems to draw us into their mood, or fast so that the lighting itself seems to be saying 'look here'. The timing you use will depend on the dramatic requirement of the particular piece.

In this exercise the court as an entity is emphasized rather then the characters. It would also be possible to show the emotional journey of Leontes, for example, much as suggested in the previous exercise.

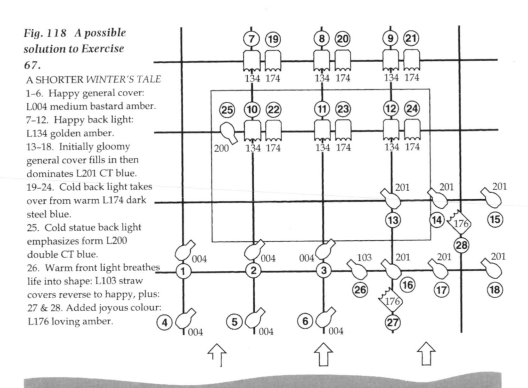

Fig. 118 *A possible solution to Exercise 67.*

A SHORTER *WINTER'S TALE*

1–6. Happy general cover: L004 medium bastard amber.

7–12. Happy back light: L134 golden amber.

13–18. Initially gloomy general cover fills in then dominates L201 CT blue.

19–24. Cold back light takes over from warm L174 dark steel blue.

25. Cold statue back light emphasizes form L200 double CT blue.

26. Warm front light breathes life into shape: L103 straw covers reverse to happy, plus:

27 & 28. Added joyous colour: L176 loving amber.

SHAKESPEARE TEXTS: FURTHER EXERCISES

The familiarity most of us have with at least some of these stories make them a very worthwhile source of project work. They are also, of course, richly atmospheric.

Macbeth
Create lighting for the first seven scenes of the play.

The Merchant of Venice
Create lighting applicable to the mood for the court scene, Act IV, incorporating a feeling of time passing.

Romeo and Juliet
Light your acting area for the following scenes:

1. The balcony scene
2. The same later, at sunrise
3. The cathedral interior
4. The tomb.

Other suitable texts: The Tempest, A Midsummer-Night's Dream, King Lear, Othello.

(See also *Hamlet* Exercise 61.)

SIMILAR TEXTS

The works of certain twentieth-century playwrights are also suitable for this sort of exercise:

The Room, The Birthday Party, The Caretaker by Harold Pinter
The Ghost Sonata by August Strindberg
Ghosts by Henrik Ibsen
Spring Awakening by Franz Wedekind

In the next exercise two short plays are given as texts that require setting in very different contexts.

EXERCISE 68
ACT WITHOUT WORDS AND *WORDS AND MUSIC*

Read *Act Without Words* and *Words and Music* by Samuel Beckett. You are required to create two distinctly different lighting states, in an area of your choosing, for these two short plays. The quotes next to each title are the director's summing up of the basic requirement for each piece.

a. *Act Without Words* – 'Dazzling light'
b. *Words and Music* – 'How much longer cooped up here in the dark?'

Analysis – Exercise 68
This exercise depends on your interpretation of the text. Whilst I offer my own solution (*see* Fig. 119) it is not to suggest I am right or that there is a single definitive answer. My solution should be compared with your own to see how we have addressed the problems of the text in different ways.

Looking at the work of other designers should feed back into our own work. We grow and develop as lighting designers by reacting to the work of others as much as being influenced by light we see around us in 'real' situations. We should be similarly influenced by works in other media – paintings, film and television.

Finally, we return to a more complex, abstract exercise. It is important to keep our imagination charged throughout our working lives.

EXERCISE 69
THE LIGHT FANTASTIC

Within your working space create a piece of lighting to suggest one or a number of the following themes:

a. Blues in the night
b. Conversation
c. New York
d. Yellow
e. Forests of dreams
f. The voice.

Analysis – Exercise 69
These abstract concepts have no definitive answer.

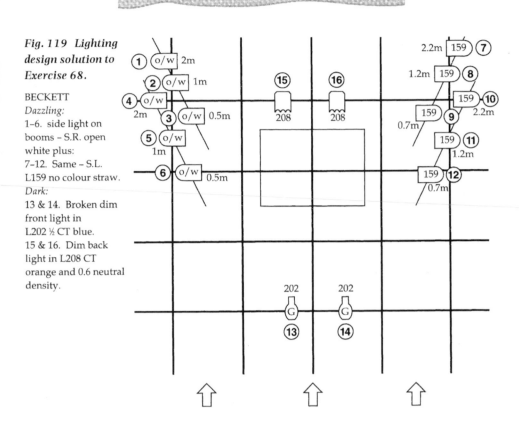

Fig. 119 Lighting design solution to Exercise 68.

BECKETT
Dazzling:
1–6. side light on booms – S.R. open white plus:
7–12. Same – S.L. L159 no colour straw.
Dark:
13 & 14. Broken dim front light in L202 ½ CT blue.
15 & 16. Dim back light in L208 CT orange and 0.6 neutral density.

TIMINGS AND PRE-HEATS

Any cue can have two timings: an 'up time' controlling circuits increasing in level, and a 'down time' controlling circuits decreasing in level. Setting these at different speeds creates a 'split timing', whereby the lighting states flow more smoothly from one to another without dipping (typical example: Up = 3 seconds, Down = 10 seconds) or deliberately creating a dip to mark scene divisions (typical example: Up = 7 seconds, Down = 1 second). The pre-heat also helps in this way. It is created by plotting into the previous cue units at an imperceptible level (for example, 10–20 per cent), so that on executing the cue they appear sooner in the fade than they would otherwise.

TOPICS FOR SIMILAR EXERCISES

a. Faustus
b. Life and death
c. Famine
d. The Blues
e. Hopscotch
f. Eggs and bacon
g. Iceberg
h. The Sudan
i. The deepest purple
j. Anti-climax
k. Lost horizon
l. Shakespeare
m. That sinking feeling
n. Snakes and ladders

Setting such exercises for each other and seeing the results can be almost as much fun as doing them!

SUMMARY

In this chapter we have really matured as lighting designers. Our ideas about effective lighting, the painting of attractive, dramatically relevant pictures with light now also relate to, and derive from, the written word – the text of the play itself. The more we practise these skills in exercises and on real stages, the broader our experience becomes and the more effective we will be as lighting designers.

The next aspect of the work of the lighting designer that we must look at is the manner in which our work fits into the production process generally. This forms the next chapter.

13

THE PRODUCTION PROCESS – RIGGING, FOCUSING, PLOTTING, THE DIRECTOR

'In Action, How Like an Angel!'

The exercises we have carried out in this book have all been in preparation for lighting a dramatic piece on stage. Working with colleagues in a studio or classroom space is not the same as working alongside a director and designer to create a finished production that will go in front of a paying audience. The next exercises are aimed at developing a good understanding of working practices.

EXERCISE 70
WORKING IN THE THEATRE SPACE

The following events all form part of the production process – the exercise here is to put them in correct chronological order. If you are not sure of what any one of them means look at the definitions overleaf explaining the list below.

1. Production meeting
2. Final run-through
3. Dress rehearsal
4. First night
5. LX plotting session
6. Focusing session
7. LX rigging session
8. Technical rehearsal
9. Reading the play
10. Stagger-through
11. Get-in
12. Get-out
13. Last night
14. Equipment hire
15. Preview
16. Read-through
17. Fit-up
18. Run-through
19. Sound plotting

Definition of Aspects of the Theatre Process

Fig. 120 *Working in the theatre space. The technical rehearsal.*

1. *Production meeting* Often before rehearsals have started, the entire technical team meets with the director and designer to form an understanding of the production style and to take an initial look at the set, costume designs, and so on. All departments discuss any problems arising.

2. *Final run-through* A complete run of the production in the rehearsal room at the end of the rehearsal process.

3. *Dress rehearsal* Full rehearsal on stage with full technical facilities, costumes, and so on. There are usually three DR's before the opening of a standard production.

4. *First night* The first performance of the production before a paying audience, usually with critics in attendance.

5. *LX plotting session* The lighting states are created on stage and plotted into the lighting board by the operator. The lighting designer, the director (and usually the designer) are present. The cues are put into the cuing script, 'the book', by the deputy stage manager.

6. Focusing session The lighting designer directs the light from each unit to where he or she wants it. The lighting designer usually stays on the ground and directs the lighting crew who do the actual physical work.

7. LX rigging session The lighting crew put the equipment into place in the theatre.

8. Technical rehearsal With the full technical team and cast present, the play is worked through with the express purpose of rehearsing all the technical cues such as scene changes, lighting, and sound. Where possible the text may be skipped – a 'cue-to-cue'.

9. Reading the play Reading through the script that is to be staged.

10. Stagger-through A run-through at an early stage of the rehearsals.

11. Get-in Getting the equipment and scenery into the theatre space and/or putting up the set itself.

12. Get-out Getting the equipment and scenery out of the theatre space and/or taking down the set and lighting rig.

13. Last night The final performance of the play.

14. Equipment hire Ordering any lighting equipment to be hired for the production.

15. Preview A performance to an audience prior to the first night to allow for final adjustments to be made before the critics see the production. Not all productions have previews.

16. Read-through Usually the first day of rehearsals, when the actors read their parts out aloud. Technicians and designers are often invited.

17. Fit-up The stage is made ready for the production. The 'fit-up' usually describes the period when the set/scenery is built or put together on stage, but can also apply to rigging and the like.

18. Run-through A rehearsal of the play from start to finish, without stopping. A production may have any number of run-throughs.

19. Sound plotting The sound cues are established in the theatre space, levels set, and so on. The director and technicians are present. The cues are put into the cuing script, 'the book', by the deputy stage manager.

Analysis – Exercise 70
Although some events can occur at different times, the correct sequence would generally be as follows:

9. Reading the play Essential first step.

1. Production meeting Gets everybody on track.

16. Read-through First day of rehearsals.

10. Stagger-through Often the only chance to see the whole thing before committing to the design.

18. Run-through A chance to see the play rehearsed in sequence.

14. Equipment hire Has to be done fairly early to guarantee they have what you want.

2. Final run-through Useful for confirmation of lighting design and to help refine a cue synopsis.

11. Get-in Getting it all there.

7. LX rigging session Getting it all in place.

17. Fit-up Can often coincide with or precede the rigging.

6. Focusing session Getting it all working correctly.

5. LX plotting session Creating the lighting.

19. Sound plotting Creating the sound.

8. Technical rehearsal Rehearsing the lighting.

3. Dress rehearsal Practising the lighting.

15. Preview Performing/refining the lighting.

OTHER SUCH TERMS

1. *Zitsprobe:* a static rehearsal (often sitting down) for musicians and singers in an opera production.
2. *Piano rehearsal:* an opera rehearsal without full orchestra.
3. *Orchestra get-in:* the musicians move into the theatre with their instruments and equipment.
4. *Costume parade:* a showing of the costumes to the director – often under the lighting that will be used.
5. *Fight call:* specific rehearsal of a stage fight sequence.
6. *Pyrotechnics call:* specific rehearsal of a pyrotechnical sequence.
7. *Fire inspection:* local authority licensing officer checks the safety of the production.
8. *Photo call/Press call:* cast required on stage to meet the press!

(*See also* Viewing the Model, page 139.)

4. First night Performing the lighting.

13. Last night Final performance.

12. Get-out Putting it all away as necessary.

SCHEDULING

For financial reasons, theatres are kept 'dark' (not open to the public) for as short a period as possible, so set-up time in the theatre space can be very limited. In order to streamline the process and keep everything on track, a production schedule is usually made. Every production has different needs and therefore its own unique schedule, but it is worth looking at a couple of examples to see how they are generally laid out.

EXERCISE 71
THE PRODUCTION SCHEDULE

Take the following list of production events and put them in correct chronological order:

1. Fit-up
2. Scene painting
3. LX plotting
4. Rigging
5. Fire inspection
6. Get-in
7. Props get-in
8. Set-up for technical rehearsal
9. Dress rehearsal #1
10. Dress rehearsal #2
11. Dress rehearsal #3
12. First night
13. Costume parade
14. Technical rehearsal
15. Technical work as required (derived from notes)
16. Sound get-in
17. Director's notes to actors
18. Director's notes to technicians/ designers
19. Sound plotting.

Analysis – Exercise 71

A glance at a typical production schedule for a medium-sized production shows the correct order of the elements in this process. The first example is of an 'in-house' production and the second a touring venue.

Production Schedule 1

Day One (Sunday)
9.30 am   Get into theatre – fit up set
1.00 pm   Lunch
2.00 pm   Continue fit-up – LX and sound rig FOH
6.00 pm   Evening break
7.00 pm   Continue fit-up–LX and sound rig on stage
10.00 pm Call ends

Day Two (Monday)
9.30 am   LX focus
1.00 pm   Lunch
2.00 pm   LX focus
6.00 pm   Evening break
7.00 pm   Sound plotting/scenic painting on stage
10.00 pm Call ends

Day Three (Tuesday)
9.30 am   LX plotting/props get-in
1.00 pm   Lunch
2.00 pm   LX plotting/set-up for tech
5.30 pm   Evening break
6.30 pm   Costume parade
7.30 pm   Technical rehearsal starts
10.00 pm Call ends
(For definitions of the terms used above, *see* overleaf.)

Day Four (Wednesday)

9.30 am	Technical rehearsal
1.00 pm	Lunch
2.00 pm	Technical rehearsal
5.00 pm	Fire inspection
5.30 pm	Evening break
6.30 pm	Set-up for dress rehearsal
7.30 pm	Dress rehearsal
9.30 pm	Notes
10.30 pm	Call ends

Day Five (Thursday)

9.30 am	Technical work as necessary
12.30 pm	Lunch
1.30 pm	Set-up for dress rehearsal
2.00 pm	Dress rehearsal #2
5.00 pm	Notes
6.00 pm	Evening break
7.00 pm	Set-up for performance
7.30 pm	First night

LIGHTING TERMS

LX Lighting/Electrics
FOH Front of House. For example, rigging FOH = above the audience not the stage.

Of course there are many variations on this theme. In order to open a day earlier, the set fit-up, light and sound rigging, and focusing and plotting are often scheduled to go through the night. This schedule has the set-up for the performance, the 'tech', beginning at 7.30 pm which is less than ideal as everyone will

be tired by then. Sound and light plotting will need to be longer if the production has a great number of cues. As a lighting designer you must always be well prepared, as so much depends on the efficiency and clear thinking of the technicians, designers and the director.

The following production schedule is for a touring production, and shows just how tight a schedule can be.

Production Schedule 2

9.00 am	Get into theatre, fit-up set, LX and sound
12.00	Sound, lunch, fire inspection
1.00 pm	LX lunch/sound, plot
2.00 pm	LX focus and plot
4.00 pm	Actors arrive, 'cue-to-cue' tech'
6.00 pm	Evening break
7.00 pm	Set-up for performance
8.00 pm	First night

Several things are implied in this schedule: the set is made to go together quickly and no painting is required; the lighting is an adaptation of the rig already in-house, or has been previously prepared; and the lighting states are being brought in to be loaded into a new control and then adapted for the particular space. It is very likely that the lighting designer will not be present and somebody else, often the company manager, will be responsible for 're-lighting' the show. The actors know their parts, and with no need for a full dress rehearsal, they simply have to orientate themselves to the new space. In such a tight schedule it is very important that the technicians and the person designated to re-light know exactly what they are doing.

We must understand the working practices developed over the years to allow for the smooth transition from rehearsal room to stage. You will already be familiar with some of the sessions, such as focusing and plotting, but even these take on a different aspect when you find yourself in charge or part of a bigger technical team.

The next exercises look at the most important of these sessions and aim to help develop the necessary skills to make the best use of the limited time in the theatre space.

DEVELOPING THE DESIGN

Creating a lighting design involves many elements. The exercises in this book so far have been mostly aimed at expanding your ability to create lighting scenarios developed from interpreting text, discussion with director and designer, and seeing a run-through in rehearsal.

Lighting designers get their ideas in many different ways and it is a good thing to develop a number of strategies to help you work creatively. If you only develop a single method, such as seeing a good run-through of the play, you will come unstuck when circumstances thwart you and the director decides not to do a run! Even if you do have a run to attend this may be in a dingy rehearsal room, on a floor a different size to the real stage, and on a cold, wet Wednesday morning when you are feeling particularly uninspired. Nevertheless, this may be your only chance, so you need to be able to concentrate on the matter in hand. Make sure you arrive for the run with a good understanding of how the set and costumes will look. Also make sure that you know where the actual stage areas are represented in the rehearsal room. Ask the stage manager if anything is missing, for example, high platforms may not be obvious in the rehearsal room layout.

'Imagine' the set into the rehearsal space and the costumes on to the actors. During the run concentrate both on where the action is taking place and on the dramatic mood of the moment. Interpret this in your head into the visual effect you want to create and be sure to take good notes – maybe on the script itself, or on a series of photocopied sketches of the stage design plan. At first you may need to see several runs to get a clear idea of what you want the lighting to do, but you should aim to be able to do this from just one run – as this is often all you get!

Through this process of watching rehearsals and having discussions with the director and designer you will eventually arrive at a definitive list of what you need to create the lighting design. These decisions have to be made so that ideas can be brought into being. The best way to do this is to make a list, in order of importance, of the elements required by the production. You should then work through it and decide what equipment, placed where, and in what colour, is going to be used to make each element work. You may have to work through the list several times, testing one idea against another, changing priorities, shifting the use of equipment, and so on. It may be useful to go back to previous exercises, or options within exercises that you did not use, to try putting ideas on paper. It would be particularly useful to work from a text, list your ideas, and then prioritize them.

It is right that the lighting designer should be ambitious in his or her lighting plans and it can be frustrating to find that, in practice, compromise is almost always necessary either for technical or financial reasons.

To summarize: the importance of reading the text, taking good notes, watching rehearsals and discussion with others involved in the production process, cannot be over-emphasized.

DRAWING THE PLAN

A professional lighting design is drawn on paper. It is a document aimed at achieving the rig, it does not tell anyone what the actual lighting will look like. Although lighting designers may make notes to remind themselves of what some of the units are doing, the lighting stays, for the most part, in the lighting designer's head.

The lighting designer, working on a drawing board, will be placing the equipment on to a drawing that combines the set design plan with a plan of the theatre layout. Designers use stencils to create the luminaire shapes which leaves the rest of the drawing as simply a number of straight lines, so no great technical drawing skills are needed. It is more important that the plan is clear and can be easily worked from by the rigging team. There are also a number of highly useable Computer Aided Design (CAD) packages dedicated to the drawing and analysis of such designs.

A side-elevation of the stage space will help the lighting designer to locate the equipment on the plan so that it will function successfully in the three-dimensional space. A visit to the theatre before, during and after drawing the plan to check that the positions shown on the plan will work, could be considered essential.

It is often the case that the initial design is drawn on a transparency – the lighting designer puts the set and theatre plans underneath the transparency, adds the equipment on top and then copies through all the

Fig. 121 Drawing the plan.

relevant information. The design is always prepared in this order so that the luminaires can be seen above any intersecting lines. These are then copied on to paper for distribution.

The next exercise includes an example of such a plan.

EXERCISE 72
DRAWING THE PLAN

Look at the lighting plan in Fig. 122. The drawing is finished but not all the relevant information has been added.

a. Make a list of the additional information you would you expect the plan to carry.
b. Make a list of any other paperwork you would expect the lighting designer to produce, deriving from the lighting design plan.

Analysis – Exercise 72
a. Completed lighting design – 'Hush' (Fig. 123, page 178).

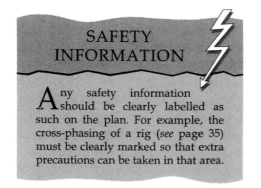

COLOUR LABELLING

It may be important to identify the colour manufacturer as most have numbers in common – although many number ranges imply the manufacturer.

The following abbreviations are used: Lee = L, Gam = G, Rosco = #.

b. Other paperwork – *See* Fig. 124 pages 180–1.

Circuit Field
Colour Call
Cue Synopsis
Cue Sheet
Focus Plot
Equipment List

FOCUSING

An important part of the production process for the lighting designer is the focusing session – even the best plan on paper can only produce great lighting if the focusing and then the plotting are carried out efficiently.

In the exercises up to this point you have been able to choose whether to focus your own rig, or use someone else to focus for you as is more often the practice in a theatre of any reasonable size. If you have not been working in this way then it is worth practising your ability to communicate clearly

SAFETY INFORMATION

Any safety information should be clearly labelled as such on the plan. For example, the cross-phasing of a rig (*see* page 35) must be clearly marked so that extra precautions can be taken in that area.

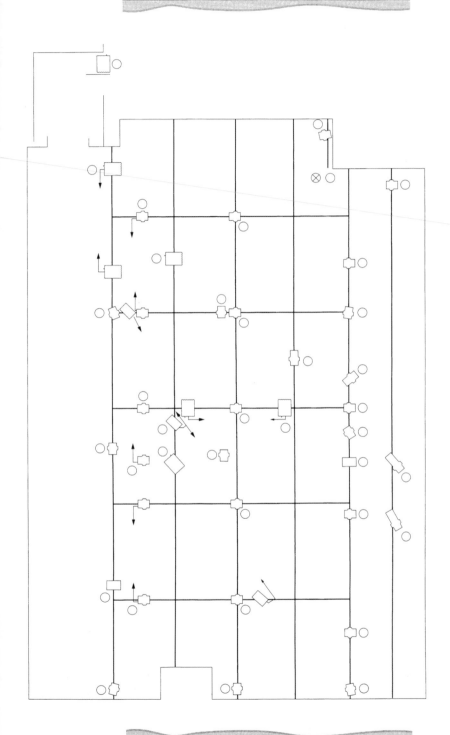

Fig. 122 The bare bones of a drawn lighting design. What is missing?

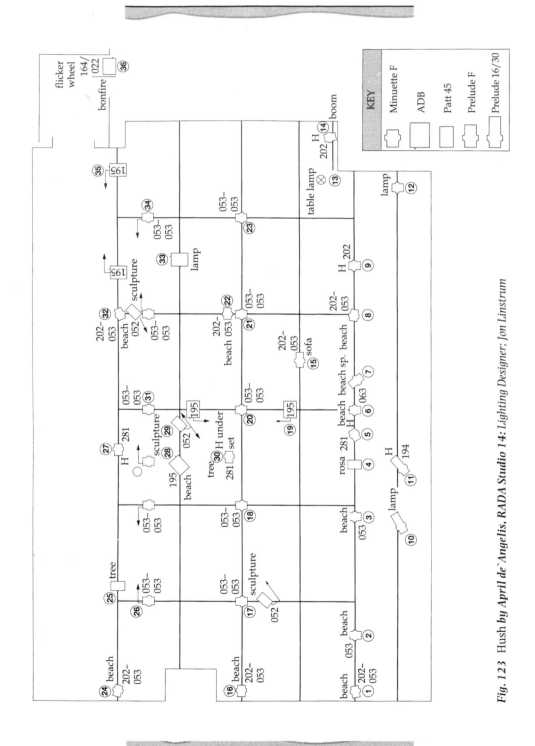

Fig. 123 Hush by April de'Angelis, RADA Studio 14: Lighting Designer: Jon Linstrum

with the focuser by carrying out one of the exercises listed below.

EXERCISE 73
FOCUSING WITH A TEAM

Use one of the following exercises that you have not already tried, and fulfil the requirements of the exercise using a second person to focus the units for you. The focusing tips in the box on page 93 should help you.

Exercises 39, 41 and 50–3.

Analysis – Exercise 73
It is important to develop good communication skills and an ability to work quickly and decisively. It is also important that you develop the ability to put the light where you want it from the perspective you will have to adopt – do not just focus to the floor but to actor height. Also, you must be sure to avoid light going where you do not want it, by shuttering away spill and any other extraneous light.

PLOTTING

As indicated above, even the best design can be 'lost' at the plotting session. The plotting session is where each lighting state is created and recorded for future playback on stage in performance. The director and usually the designer will be present, and a member of the stage management team (usually the deputy stage manager) will put the cues into the cuing script, 'the book' (*see* plotting, page 168).

For plotting you need to have a good understanding of the lighting control that you will be using. So take time out well before the session to get a good working knowledge of what it will and will not allow you to do. Even if, as is often the case, you are not operating it yourself, a good grasp of the lighting board's functions and potential will stand you in good stead.

The next exercise will give you the opportunity to stretch yourself in using the control board presently at your disposal.

EXERCISE 74
PLOTTING PRACTICE 1

Choose a recording of a piece of music, listen to it and design lighting to accompany it – *son et lumière*. Before proceeding note the following:

a. Even very short pieces of music can require many units, so be careful not to over-reach yourself. Slow tempo pieces are easier.

b. It is easier to light something rather than an empty space, so put an object into your area – something large but abstract, such as a pile of chairs covered by a white sheet, will feature the lighting without being a distraction.

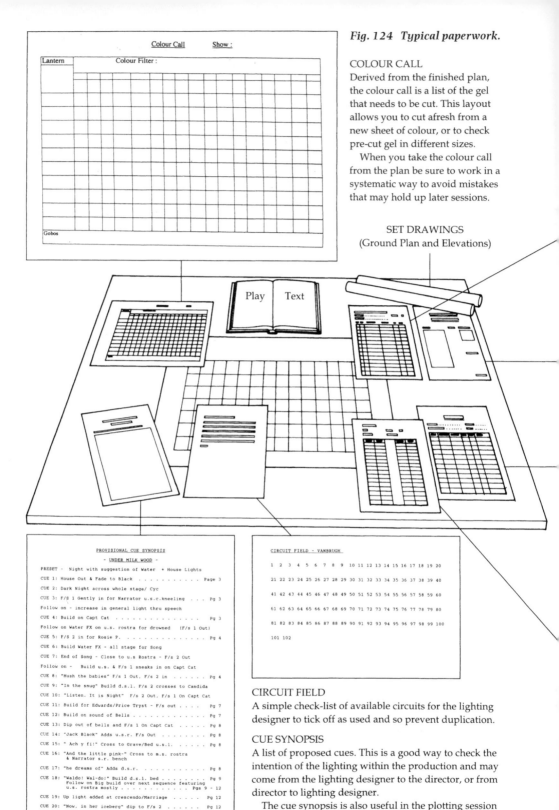

Fig. 124 Typical paperwork.

COLOUR CALL
Derived from the finished plan, the colour call is a list of the gel that needs to be cut. This layout allows you to cut afresh from a new sheet of colour, or to check pre-cut gel in different sizes.

When you take the colour call from the plan be sure to work in a systematic way to avoid mistakes that may hold up later sessions.

SET DRAWINGS
(Ground Plan and Elevations)

Colour Call   Show :

Lantern   Colour Filter :

Gobos

Play | Text

CIRCUIT FIELD
A simple check-list of available circuits for the lighting designer to tick off as used and so prevent duplication.

CUE SYNOPSIS
A list of proposed cues. This is a good way to check the intention of the lighting within the production and may come from the lighting designer to the director, or from director to lighting designer.

The cue synopsis is also useful in the plotting session to provide a quick reference to cue numbers.

```
              PROVISIONAL CUE SYNOPSIS

                - UNDER MILK WOOD -

PRESET -  Night with suggestion of Water  + House Lights

CUE 1: House Out & Fade to Black . . . . . . . . . . . Page 3

CUE 2: Dark Night across whole stage/ Cyc

CUE 3: F/S 1 Gently in for Narrator u.s.c.kneeling . . . Pg 3

Follow on - increase in general light thru speech

CUE 4: Build on Capt Cat . . . . . . . . . . . . .  Pg 3

Follow on Water FX on u.s. rostra for drowned   (F/s 1 Out)

CUE 5: F/S 2 in for Rosie P. . . . . . . . . . . . . . Pg 4

CUE 6: Build Water FX - all stage for Song

CUE 7: End of Song - Close to u.s Rostra - F/s 2 Out

Follow on -   Build u.s. & F/s 1 sneaks in on Capt Cat

CUE 8: "Hush the babies" F/s 1 Out, F/s 2 in . . . . . . Pg 4

CUE 9: "In the snug" Build d.s.l. F/s 2 crosses to Candida

CUE 10: "Listen. It is Night" F/s 2 Out, F/s 1 On Capt Cat

CUE 11: Build for Edwards/Price Tryst - F/s out . . . .  Pg 7

CUE 12: Build on sound of Bells . . . . . . . . . . . . Pg 7

CUE 13: Dip out of bells and F/s On Capt Cat . . . . . Pg 8

CUE 14: "Jack Black" Adds u.s.r. F/s Out . . . . . . . . Pg 8

CUE 15: " Ach y fi!" Cross to Grave/Bed u.s.l. . . . . . Pg 8

CUE 16: "And the little pink-" Cross to m.s. rostra
        & Narrator s.r. bench

CUE 17: "he dreams of" Adds d.s.r. . . . . . . . . . . . Pg 8

CUE 18: "Waldo! Wal-do!" Build d.s.l. bed . . . . . . . Pg 9
        Follow on Big build over next sequence featuring
        u.s. rostra mostly . . . . . . . . . . . . Pgs 9 - 12

CUE 19: Up light added at crescendo/Marriage . . . . . Pg 12

CUE 20: "Now, in her iceberg" dip to F/s 2 . . . . . . Pg 12

CUE 21: Cross to Bed d.s.l. (F/s out) . . . . . . . . . Pg 13

CUE 22: "In butcher Beynon s" d.s.r & F/S 1 . . . . . . Pg 14
```

```
        CIRCUIT FIELD - VANBRUGH

1  2  3  4  5  6  7  8  9  10 11 12 13 14 15 16 17 18 19 20

21 22 23 24 25 26 27 28 29 30 31 32 33 34 35 36 37 38 39 40

41 42 43 44 45 46 47 48 49 50 51 52 53 54 55 56 57 58 59 60

61 62 63 64 65 66 67 68 69 70 71 72 73 74 75 76 77 78 79 80

81 82 83 84 85 86 87 88 89 90 91 92 93 94 95 96 97 98 99 100

101 102
```

CUE SHEET

The list of cues made during the plotting session that the lighting operator works from.

A separate cue sheet would be used to operate a follow spot, or carry out any stage electrics duties such as operating a smoke machine or pyrotechnics.

LANTERN STOCK & TECHNICAL DETAILS

FOCUS PLOT

A list of luminaires and their use on stage. This is usually created after the first night as a guide to refocusing if the units are accidentally moved. Essential for a touring rig.

PATCHING SHEET
See Patching, page 29.

Analysis – Exercise 74

This becomes an exercise in many things: interpretation of text (in this case the music); the use of abstract light to suggest mood; colour and shape; texture and angle. You may also wish to use motion effects (*see* Chapter 9).

This exercise is also about getting the lighting to flow with the music through the fine tuning of the control equipment. It will require precise timings and/or operation of cues (*see* Timings box, page 162).

The next exercise adds the other feature of a plotting session that may need careful handling – the director!

THE DIRECTOR

Throughout the production process the lighting designer will need to have developed a good working relationship with the director. This comes to a climax in the plotting session, when what has so far been only talked about becomes reality. Good communication skills, tact, diplomacy and forward planning all come into play. The following two exercises are designed to help you gain confidence in this area.

EXERCISE 75
PLOTTING PRACTICE 2

a. Repeat Exercise 74, but on this occasion have the piece of music chosen for you.

b. Ask the person choosing the music to suggest the moods and concepts to be illustrated in your lighting.

c. Have the other person plot the lighting alongside you either as director (if they can 'play' this role), or simply as another person whose opinions should count.

The box below contains a list of music that I have found very useful for this exercise in the past.

SON ET LUMIÈRE SUGGESTIONS

Copland, *Clarinet Concerto*, opening section.
Ravel, *Piano Concerto*, 2nd movement.
Copland, *Fanfare for the Common Man*.
Barber, *Adagio*.
Shostokovich, *Symphony No. 5*, opening section.
Vaughan Williams, *Symphonia Antarctica*, closing section.

Analysis – Exercise 75

If you are used to creating lighting from these exercises or working in such a way that you can usually please yourself, it can come as quite a shock to suddenly have to work to the creative ideas of another. But all theatre is essentially a collaborative art form and as such it is essential that you should get used to working in this way.

A number of things are particularly important here, and they apply to all the parties involved:

a. That we listen to the ideas of others with an open mind.
b. That we do not cling to our own ideas simply because they are ours.
c. That we create the best possible lighting for the production regardless of whose idea it is.
d. That we continue to be open to new ideas, even up to the last minute.
e. That our mastery of the technical aspects of the job frees us to be as creative as possible.

Plotting with input from others is difficult to practise. In a real situation, when a show has to be put together from so many elements, the director will have a million other distractions and worries.

EXERCISE 76
PLOTTING PRACTICE 3

Use either an old exercise, the new one below, or one of your own devising and ask another person to undertake the role of director.

To the Director
Your colleague needs to experience the pressure of working alongside a director who is difficult to please, so set out to make it as hard as possible to achieve a finished piece of lighting. The light-ing itself need not be technically difficult, or the rig large, but your demands should be very precise and exacting. Here are a few things to try:

a. Keep changing your mind – ask for a piece of lighting to be set as dark as possible and then decide you want it very bright.
b. Whilst retaining a clear idea of what you mean to get out of the lighting, express your thoughts using obscure words and phrases (for example, 'I need a esoterically miasmic quality to this piece of lighting'), so that the lighting designer must question your words until your needs are clearly understood.
c. Ask the lighting designer to do things that, on the face of it, seem impossible. You could, for example, ask for the lighting to be spectacular but very, very dark, or for the feeling of lots of colour without using gels. Make the lighting designer work hard to fulfil your needs.

These exercises only really work well with an element of role-play. If you are lucky enough to have someone who can do this well then try some of the following :

d. Try to encourage poor results by being bored and uninterested in the lighting and by asking the lighting designer to light as quickly as possible.

e. Be easily distracted – talk to other people in the room or about anything other than the lighting so that the lighting designer has to work hard to keep on track.

f. Tell the lighting designer one thing – take some time to brief him or her – but secretly try and get something completely different out of the lighting.

NEW EXERCISE THE PICNIC

Having been given your performance area, create a lighting state to suggest a clearing in a wood. It is a warm, sunny afternoon in midsummer in the south of England.

a. A 'pre-set' suggesting the mood to come.

b. The main state as described above.

c. Later – clouds are now blocking the sun – it is slightly duller and cooler.

d. A 'post-set' – suggesting the cooler mood of the last state.

It is important that the lighting on the actor appears the same at any given point within the area.

Analysis – Exercise 76
Working with a director (and/or designer) can be most challenging and rewarding. Creating a good working partnership and taking this through a number of productions is particularly good experience, and usually produces the best work.

SUMMARY

This chapter has endeavoured to show you the manner in which the skills of the lighting designer are brought to the theatre. All will be lost if the designer does not have the means to translate his or her own vision on to the stage. The techniques and methods discussed in this chapter could be of use whether working alone or on a big production; in a studio or in an opera house.

With them as part of your repertoire you are now ready to proceed in your work as a lighting designer.

14

LIGHTING DESIGN EXAMPLES

'Example Is the School of Mankind'

Finally, here are a few lighting design ground-plans to mull over as examples of a finished product. They are all plans that I saw through to fruition: all became real lighting on successful productions. It is all very well to theorize about lighting and carry out exercises to stimulate ideas and to learn from, but a finished lighting design is much more real. It will be useful for you to study the plans which I have annotated to include all the idiosyncrasies and errors of a real design. I have also included the cue synopsis and/or scene breakdowns.

The next exercise outlines how to study a lighting plan.

EXERCISE 77
LIGHTING DESIGN STUDIES

By studying the lighting plans in detail, work out the following:

a. How is the general cover put together?
b. What units are being used for specials?
c. Are there any colour or gobo washes in use?
d. What is the general tone of colour in use?
e. What, if any, special effects are being used?
f. How does the lighting designer address the set?
g. Do you think this plan would have worked well?

Analysis – Exercise 77

What becomes interesting from analysing these designs is whether any sense of my own personal lighting style is apparent. Notice that as a way of spreading the equipment I am fond of the one-sided cover. I like to include a dark blue (#79) from the front to colour in shadows and double for night. It is probably already obvious from the design exercises that there are certain colours and ideas that I know to work and fall back on time after time. With experience, you will also develop these instincts.

UNDER MILK WOOD BY DYLAN THOMAS

This production in the Mermaid Theatre, London, shows a typical rig for a wide proscenium theatre with a shallow thrust.

The set by Saul Radomsky – a giant graveyard – is further framed with a cyclorama for cloud projection viewed through an oval mask with small, cut-out houses in silhouette along its lower edge. It opened up some very exciting lighting opportunities (*see* Fig. 125 for photograph of set model).

General Description of the Lighting

The lighting had to move the day through twenty-four hours. The sun rises stage-right and sets stage-left. Follow spots are used to subtly follow the narrator in the early, dark night-time scenes. Do not fall into using follow spots too often as a substitute for thinking through rigged specials – the follow spot has its own 'flavour' and should only be used when artistically correct. Specials are used to mark areas such as houses or to highlight individuals. Animation wheels provide the rippling water effect for the scenes of the 'drowned'. The cyc' is lit with projected moving clouds and varying degrees of blue.

Fig. 125 Set model for Under Milk Wood.

Lighting Design Analysis

CIRCUIT NOS.	DESCRIPTION OF USE	COLOUR USED
3–7, 15–18, 21, 22–25	General cover – from stage-left side only	103, 443
1 & 2	Stage-right fill for cover during day	159
30, 35, 38, 49, 60, 63, 75	Dark blue back light for night scenes	# 79
88, 90, 93, 97	Cross light from stage-right for night-time	174
41, 43, 48, 55, 58, 66–71, 94, 95	Sunrise from stage-right (C68 across height of set – i.e. cross)	212, 443, 007 mixed
27, 32, 37, 42, 46, 50, 52, 62, 64	Warm midday sun – back light	204, 236, 020
98, 99, 100–102	Stage-left side lights – start in moonlight colour, change in interval to sunset colour	174 to 134
84 & 85	Units on floor to represent sun setting	105, 158
79-82	sun across cyc'	
83	Cyc' lit from above and below in various blues	#79, 132
83	Cyc' lit from floor for dawn	194
72, 78	Cloud effects projected on cyc'	
86, 87	Moonbox and stars hung behind cyc' (using fairy lights stuck to back of cyc' for stars – *see* box below)	
103–107	Lights in house windows.	
11, 12	Follow spots	
8–10, 96	Animation effects for 'drowned' scenes	219/241 split
89, 92	Gobo dressing on cross – night and day	174, 103
86, 87	Up light from under rostra on stage floor level.	201
74	Pink wash for dream sequence	111

All other channels are specials.

MOON AND STARS

An enclosed box with an aperture through which the light from discrete sources (often household bulbs) can be seen is called a light box. With a moon-shaped aperture it becomes a moonbox and is usually placed behind a cyc'.

Stars can be simply done by hanging fairy lights so that the wire between them is unseen. Fibre optics can also be used to create this effect - when woven into a cloth this becomes a starcloth.

Fig. 126 Completed lighting design ground plan of Under Milk Wood.

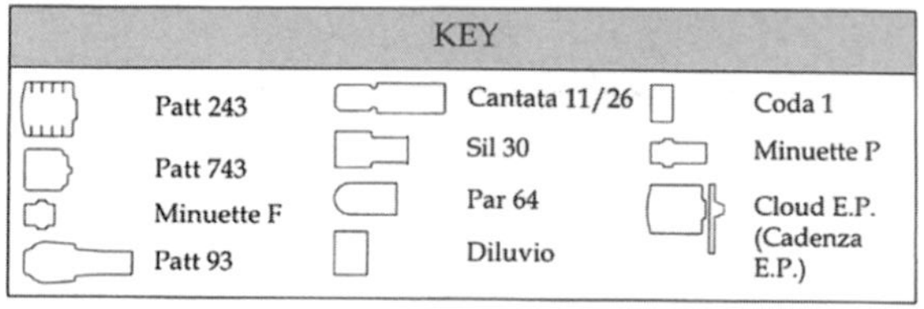

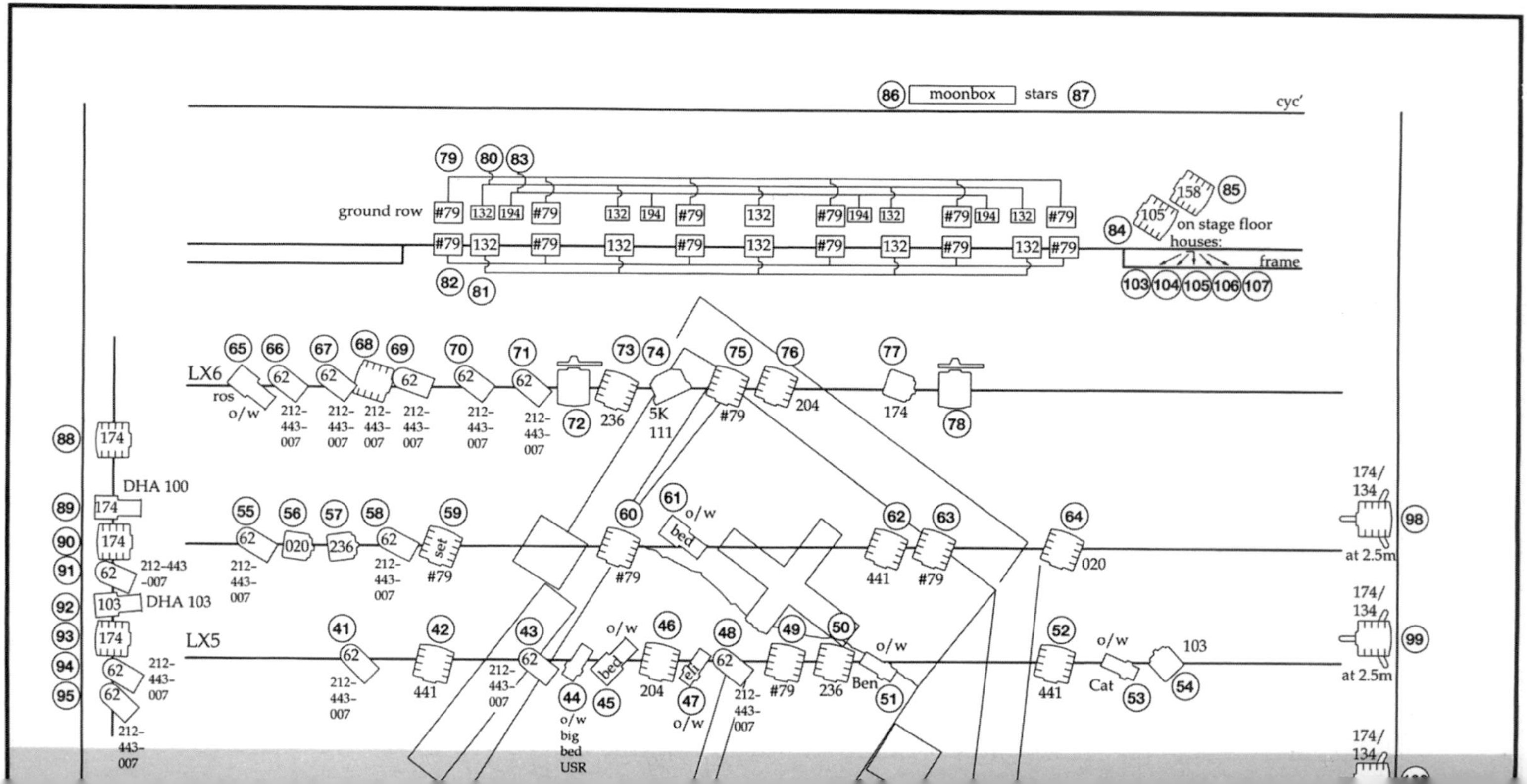

188

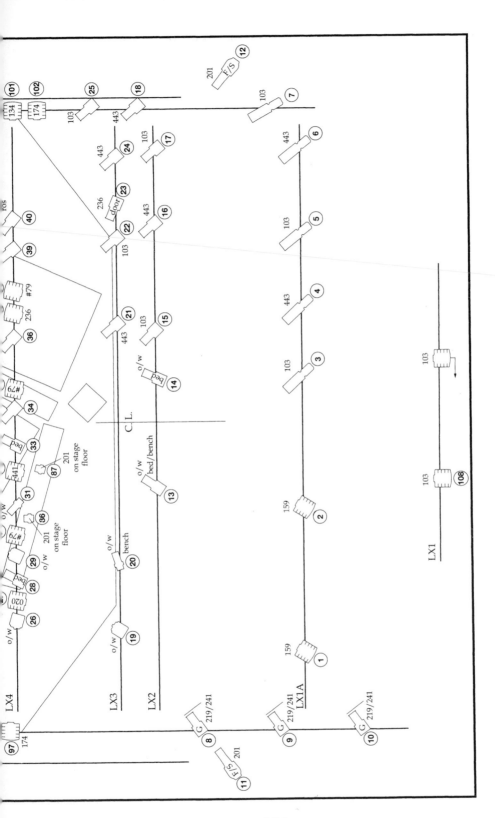

189

LIGHTING DESIGN EXAMPLES

Cue Synopsis

PRESET – Night with suggestion of water and house lights

CUE 1: House out and fade to black . .Page 3

CUE 2: Dark night across whole stage/cyc'

CUE 3: F/s 1 gently in for narrator u.s.c. kneeling 3

Follow on – increase in general light through speech

CUE 4: Build on Capt Cat 3

Follow on water FX on u.s. rostra for drowned (F/s 1 out)

CUE 5: F/s 2 in for Rosie P. 4

CUE 6: Build water FX – all stage for song

CUE 7: End of song – close to u.s. rostra – F/s 2 out

Follow on – build u.s. and F/s 1 sneaks in on Capt Cat

CUE 8: 'Hush the babies' F/s 1 out, F/s 2 in 4

CUE 9: 'In the snug' build d.s.l. F/s 2 crosses to s.l.

CUE 10: 'Listen it is night' F/s 2 out, F/s 1 on Capt Cat

CUE 11: Build for Edwards/Price tryst F/s out 7

CUE 12: Build on sound of bells 7

CUE 13: Dip out of bells and F/s 1 on Capt Cat 8

CUE 14: 'Jack Black' adds u.s.r. F/s out . . .8

CUE 15: 'Ach y fi!' cross to grave/bed u.s.l. 8

CUE 16: 'And the little pink' cross to m.s. rostra and narrator s.r. bench

CUE 17: 'He dreams of' adds d.s.r. 8

CUE 18: 'Waldo! Wal-do!' build d.s.l. bed . .9
Follow on big build over next sequence featuring u.s. rostra mostly 9/12

CUE 19: Up light added at crescendo/marriage 12

CUE 20: 'Now, in her iceberg' dip to F/s 2 12

CUE 21: Cross to bed d.s.l. F/s out 13

CUE 22: 'In butcher Beynon's' d.s.r and F/s 1 14

CUE 23: 'In a paper carrier' adds w.s.c. rostra 14

CUE 24: 'Babies singing opera' big operatic build for song

LIGHTING DESIGN EXAMPLES

CUE 50: Interval setting – plus house lights	CUE 58: Moon appears – with accordion music 59
CUE 51: Fade to black-out	
	CUE 59: 'A farmer's lantern' extra light on model appears and twinkles 59
CUE 52: Act 2 – Sunny a.m. featuring up-stage rostra 33	
	CUE 60: Slow fade out of pub area . (bottom) 60
CUE 53: Build to fuller stage sunny a.m. 'busy as bees' 34	
Follow on very slow build shifting to sunny p.m. by 50	CUE 61: Darkening stage through last sequence 62
CUE 54: Slow fade starts towards sunset c 54	CUE 62: Fade to silhouette of cast plus cyc' 62
CUE 55: Slow fade to night . . . . .c 57	CUE 63: Build through last song/music . .62
CUE 56: Pub light builds from within night 58	CUE 64: Fade to black-out 62
	CUE 65: Curtain call
CUE 57: 'The windy town is a hill of windows' several windows light up in model houses 59	CUE 66: Fade to post-set and house lights

Notes: Once the sun has risen there is a big gap between cues 47 (page 19) and 48 (page 33) and the follow spots cease to be used. For the same reason there are many less cues in Act 2 than there are in Act 1.

Realizing that I had not included a dark blue night wash high enough to catch the top of the cross, I swung the top light (Circuit 59) around to catch it from the side – hence the arrow set in the symbol – and focused the other top lights to spread to cover the area it was supposed to be top lighting.

2. THE JEALOUS WIFE BY GEORGE COLMAN

This Restoration piece inspired the set designer, Vicky le Sache, to create a clever and unusual raked stage shape in the otherwise narrow width of the old Vanbrugh theatre. A rope attached to the chandelier appears to be pulling up the far corner of the stage floor, and a real sense of tension exists. Figure 127 shows the preset. Note gobo rotators shine through the chandelier.

Fig. 127 Production photo. The Jealous Wife – *preset.*

Lighting Design Analysis

CIRCUIT NOS.	DESCRIPTION OF USE	COLOUR USED
1, 2, 16	Fore-stage cover from stage-left	103
31, 21	Fore-stage cover from stage-right	285
29, 33, 81, 85, 97	Cover main stage from stage-right only	206
19, 23, 34, 70, 74–76	Side light – stage-right (warm)	103
40, 41, 71, 74	Side light – stage-right (cold)	201
20, 28, 35, 37–39, 66–68, 78, 79, 87, 88, 90	Side light from stage-left	192, 152
45, 47, 51, 54, 92, 101	Back light – main stage	238–238
44, 46, 52, 55, 57, 83	Back light – alternative #1	013
61	Back light – alternative #2	174
82, 84, 86, 93, 94	Back light – fore-stage	103–207
3, 8	Dark blue front light – night	#79
62, 63	Up-stage corridor for entrances, etc	o/w
24, 36, 49, 50, 65	Backing for doorways	201
80	Up light on lifted corner of floor	174
25, 26, 30, 42, 73	Light on flown captions (gobo)	103
48, 56, 102	Gobo rotating light through chandelier	117
91	Practical chandelier	
89, 72	Light on rope	117
58, 59, 60, 64	Added colour for epilogue	Various
All other channels are specials.		

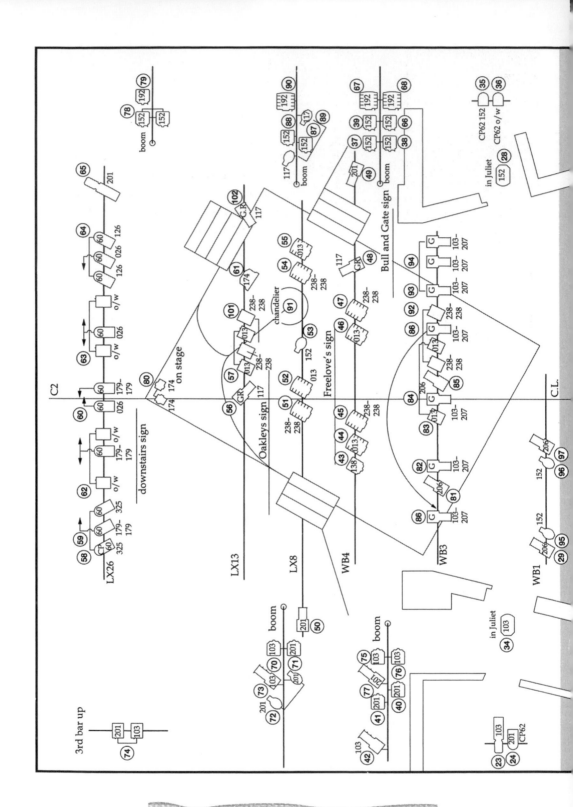

194

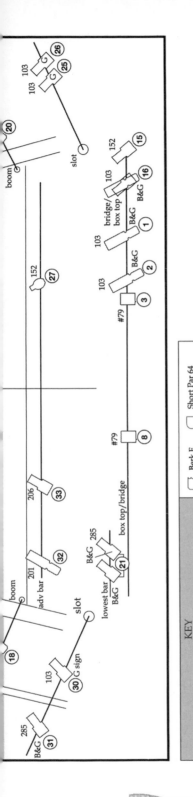

Fig. 128 Completed lighting design ground plan of The Jealous Wife.

KEY

Berk F	Short Par 64	
Minim	G = Gobo	
Bambino	GR = Gobo rotator	
	all fresnels to have barndoors	
P243 & P243 side el.	Par 64	
P743 & P743 side el.		
Polaris 261		
Sil 30 & Sil 30 side el.		
Cantata 11/26		
P23 & Cantata P.C.		

General Description of the Lighting

The lighting for this play follows the scene breakdown: there are no other cues within the scenes. The outside scenes at the Bull and Gate Inn are played on the fore-stage.

Scene Synopsis

ACT I   The Oakley house

ACT II   *Scene 1:* Bull and Gate Inn
         Scene 2: Lady Freelove's house

ACT III Lady Freelove's house

ACT IV   *Scene 1:* The Oakley house
         Scene 2: Bull and Gate Inn

ACT V   *Scene 1:* Lady Freelove's house
         Scene 2: The Oakley house

EPILOGUE

Note: Where there is not the width of lighting bar to light into the edge of the stage, a lower position on a side boom will allow the lighting designer to get the angle required nevertheless.

3. BLOODY POETRY BY HOWARD BRENTON

The CSC Theater (off Broadway) is a very open studio space. In this case the set consisted of a painted stage floor, furniture (including a grand piano) and white

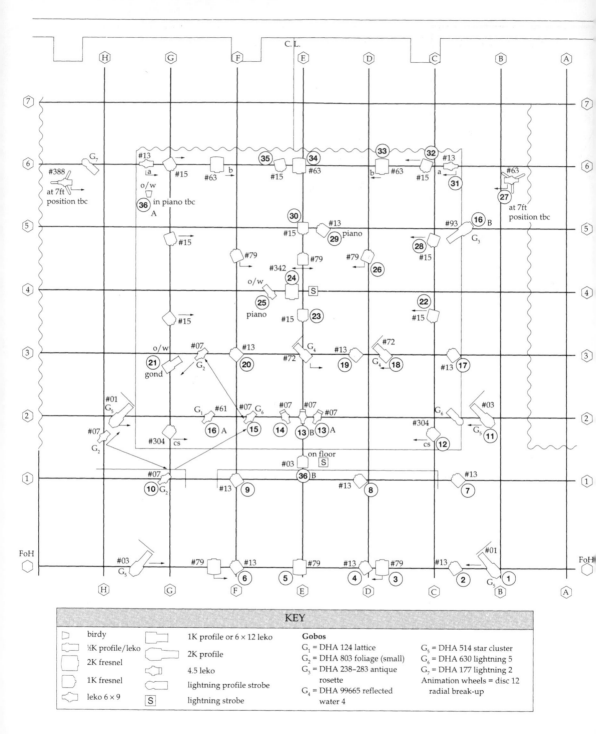

Fig. 130 Completed lighting design ground plan of Bloody Poetry.

Scene Synopsis and Notes from Discussion with Director

PRE-ACT: Piano in modern, realistic setting, costumes modern with period details/lines.
Dance.

	Scene	Notes
ACT I		
Sc 1	Coach – Bysshe	– In special (no 'flickering shadows')
Sc 2	Lake Geneva – beach a.m.	– 'looking over the lake'
		– 'brilliant light'
Sc 3	Pathways and vines	– 'bright sunshine, green leaves'
	(change of season and time from previous scene)	
Sc 4	Night	– chairs and cushions centre
		– initially intimate/cosy – window gobo?
	Polidori lights candelabra at piano	– lightning over him as he enters scene doorway
		(lightning through windows? then unreal
		interior lightning?)
	Candelabra moves	– shadows on wall
Sc 5	Bysshe alone	– special
Sc 6	Mary and Clair in room (piano) warm light	
	Men on beach	– boat and storm very dark and frightening then
		calm – Bysshe in special
ACT II		
Sc 2	England, winter	– cold garden
Sc 3	Dover beach a.m.	– Polidori narrating at piano, stormy
	(Ghost of Harriet in u.s. corridor)	
Sc 4	May, sun	– 'Blazing Light', strong back light
Sc 5:	VENICE	– 'Rippling Light' – Romantic
Sc 6:	Stained Glass	– 'Coloured Light'
	Abstract window	
Sc 7:	November – Haze	– 'Glittering Light'
	Gondolier is a pool of light with	– goes to special on Bysshe (dark) 'Stage Darkens'
	ripples around	– Shadows?
Sc 8:	Hotel Room	– 'Light' – thus darker!
Sc 9:	Hotel Room, Nov	– Special
	Main state	– 'Dreary Room'
Sc10:	BEACH – July As Act1 Sc2 but duller (sea)	
Sc11:	Polidori	– Special – 'Dark' into centre
Sc12:	A sail, Bysshe	– 'No storm effects'
		– BIG F.X. then Special c.s.
Sc13:	STORM	Shore – Fire – Still red top light for end

CURTAIN CALL – POST-SET

drapes which were hanging down like huge curtains across the up-stage edge.

The play began with the curtains extended to cover all the furniture – although set in various locations the play was in this case at all times meant to be such that the narrator was telling the story within the period drawing room revealed after the opening storm scene, and after the drapes are pulled back to reveal the furniture.

Director Chris Hayes had the curtains ripped down at the end of the play and used very dramatically to stage the drowning of Shelley sequence. The lighting had to provide all location and atmospheric detail and was thus (unusually) given a higher credit than the set

Lighting Design Analysis

CIRCUIT NOS.	DESCRIPTION OF USE	COLOUR USED
2, 4, 6, 7–9, 17, 19, 20	Front cover from stage-left only	#13
22, 23, 28, 30, 32, 35	Top/back light	#15
1, 11	Gobo cover (with effects)	#01
3, 5, 26	Dark blue wash	#79
33, 34	Moonlight back light	#63
15	Exterior gobo wash – English garden	#07
31	Dressing on back cloth	#13
?	Floor general central – up light	#03
12	Centre stage special area	#304
27	Up-stage side light for ghost	#63, #388
16B	Stained-glass window gobo – Venice	#93/#19
	Colour – four-way split	#36/#93
18	Reflected water effect – gobo and animation fx	#72
21	Special for gondola	o/w
16A	Lattice window gobo	#61
13A, 13B, 14	Specials for single people	#07
25, 29	Area around piano special	#13, o/w
36	Special for piano player	o/w
24	Centre stage red top light – end of play	#342

Notes: Working only from a conversation with the director and without knowing the theatre, I made no specific unit specification on my drawing and the US production electrician was left to choose equipment to fit my needs as demonstrated by the plan. When I arrived in New York, in time to see a run of the play, the rig was already being installed! This is why my specials radiate out from a very useful central position – at the time of drawing I had no idea where the actors would be standing for these moments!

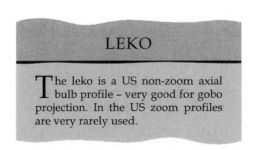

Fig. 129 Poster for the production.

LEKO

The leko is a US non-zoom axial bulb profile – very good for gobo projection. In the US zoom profiles are very rarely used.

design on the poster. Setting by Charles Townsend Wittreich Jr.

4. BEOWULF ADAPTED FOR THE STAGE BY CHRISTOPHER G. SANDFORD

A very visual production for Polka Children's theatre. Gary Thorne created a beautiful set on the main stage, a small raised proscenium with a large thrust apron, that welcomed a preponderance of gobos and extravagant colour.

SUMMARY

Studying these lighting design plans illustrate that for all the forward planning in the world a lighting design is never really finished on paper – it must adapt within the theatre space itself. As lighting designers we must remain open to the need for these adaptations.

It is debatable whether a lighting design is ever finished, even on the opening night something could probably be bettered. Nevertheless the time comes when we must move on to our next project, secure in the knowledge that the lighting we leave behind us works well for those seeing it, even if our more acute judgement sees where it could have been improved – maybe next time?

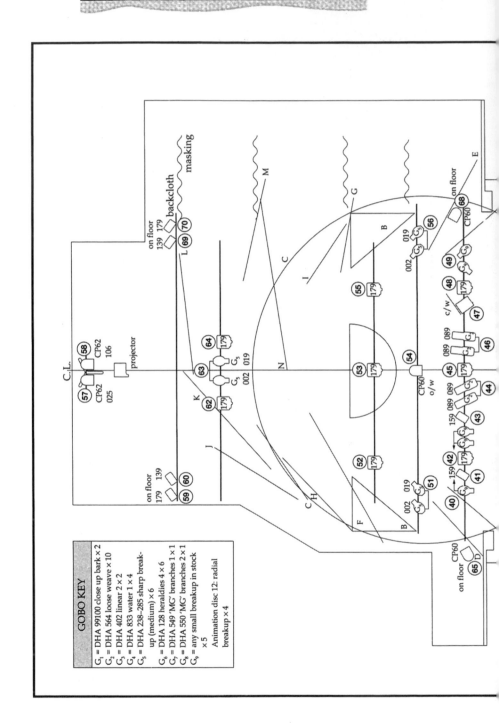

GOBO KEY

G₁ = DHA 99100 close up bark × 2
G₂ = DHA 564 loose weave × 10
G₃ = DHA 402 linear 2 × 2
G₄ = DHA 833 water 1 × 4
G₅ = DHA 238–285 sharp break-
up (medium) × 6
G₆ = DHA 128 heraldies 4 × 6
G₇ = DHA 549 'MG' branches 1 × 1
G₈ = DHA 550 'MG' branches 2 × 1
G₉ = any small breakup in stock
× 5
Animation disc 12: radial
breakup × 4

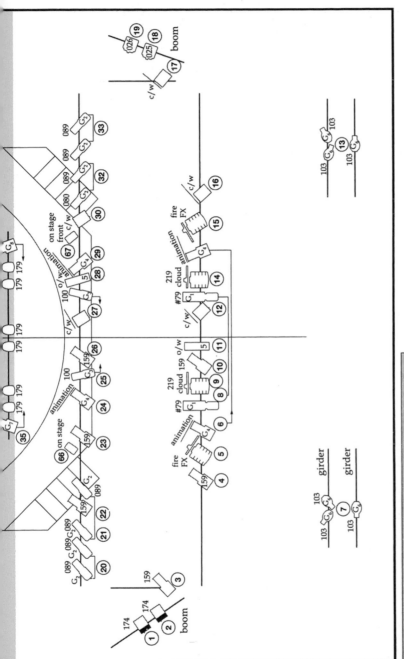

Fig. 132 Completed lighting design ground plan of Beowulf.

Fig. 131 Production photo. Beowulf, *Act I–Court.*

Lighting Design Analysis

CIRCUIT NOS.	DESCRIPTION OF USE	COLOUR USED
3, 4, 10, 22, 23, 26, 41, 43	General cover from stage-right	159
12, 16, 17, 27, 30, 47	General cover from stage-left (colour wheels)	c/w
1, 2	Cold wash from stage-right	174
18, 19	Red from stage-left – fire and sunset	
36–38, 42, 45, 48, 52, 53, 55, 62, 64	Top/back light	179
9, 14	Dark blue fill – goboed	#79
9, 14	Cloud F.X. projection	219
5, 15	Fire F.X. projection	
24, 29	Water ripple F.X.	
20, 21, 32, 33, 44, 46	Light on set – underwater/cave	089
25	Streaks on cave	100
51, 56, 63	Dragon light	002, 019
35	Barren wood	201
40	Leafy exterior	o/w
65–68	Up lighting	o/w
54	Centre stage top light special	o/w
11, 28	Specials centre stage	o/w
59, 60, 69, 70	Up light on back cloth	179, 139
57, 58	Back light on byre	025, 106
7, 13	Auditorium wall/aisle dressing: shields	103

Notes: The slide projector was used with a horizontal slit to look like a laser line – representing the surface of the sea – shone from up stage to the stage floor and then lifted as Beowulf dives under water.

LIGHTING DESIGN EXAMPLES

Scene/Cue Synopsis

PRESET – (*Note*: gobos on windows – heraldic/celtic)

ACT I: Storyteller – Quiet beginning

    COURT #1 (Warm) FANFARE
      >FIGHT – (B & Breca) > ACTION
        FREEZE(S)

    SEA – 'Blue-Green Sea' 'looks a bit cold
        & misty'
      > Diving in > Swimming Race.
      SILK FLAGS – SEA-SERPENTS –
      'Blood-red Sunset'

    COURT #1 – Celebratory Dancing
      > B & Breca alone

    SEA VOYAGE – Ship 'stars' – billowing
        cloths –
      Up light off water

    ASHORE – 'Armour shining in the sun'
      Colder sun, sunset?

    COURT #2 (Darker/Colder than court
      #1)

    DARKNESS > Chill Night > Midnight
      > GRENDEL (Slow motion)

    DAWN – Celebratory Dancing.

ACT II: COURT #2 Under threat

    JOURNEY – 'Cold, misty, eerie' >
      'twisted, gnarled trees'
      > 'blood black lake'
      > B wades into the lake (Slide/Laser
      effect) – semi-darkness – 'the
      eyes of the servants light up'

    GRENDEL'S DAM – CAVE – 'slime
      green',
      'a fire' – 'fire flares up'
      > BLOOD & GORE (Slow motion)
      >'a small hole' > 'eventually he
      saw some light'

    FOREST 'no longer dead' – Spring

    COURT #2

    SAILS HOME Quick transition

    COURT #1 – FIRE 'your great hall is on
      fire'
      Master/Slave story – Cave and
      tunnel. Chalice

    DRAGON – FLAMES (green flame?)

    FUNERAL PYRE – MORE (Different)
      FLAMES – U.S. and bigger

        -CURTAIN-

CONCLUSION

I hope you have discovered many useful things within this book. Most of all I hope that during your journey through the information and exercises in this book you have discovered the great pleasure that is to be found in working with light.

Light is a positive medium. The darkest of colours join together to create dazzling white light. The ugliest shade, which as a pigment disgusts and mortifies, becomes as a gel a vivid and vibrant hue when light passes through it. Light reflects, refracts, illuminates – in movement it sparkles, radiates and dances. Light brings to life all that it shines upon. Even the darkest light sources impart vital visual information. The shadows light produces can be mysterious, strange and enigmatic.

To make this point, one last exercise, taking us back to the most basic of artificial light sources.

Fig. 133 Reproduction of Christ Before the High Priest *by Gerit van Honthorst.*

EXERCISE 78
LAST WORDS

Within your working space reproduce the lighting shown in Fig. 133.

Place within your working space the objects shown to replicate as much as

possible the setting of this photograph.

1. Use a real candle to recreate the scene, as the painting suggests.
2. Substitute an artificial candle (if you have one) and see how effective this is. Are either enough?
3. Use a lighting rig.

NB: Actors will need to work in this space without giving away the 'cheating' light sources.

Analysis – Exercise 78

Perhaps only sunlight can really compete with the beauty of light from a real candle.

OTHER SOURCES OF INSPIRATION

As discussed (page 153) the work of great artists can inspire. These paintings in particular (all in the National Gallery in London) are worth studying, and attempting to reproduce in your theatre space:

St Francis in Meditation
            Francisco de Zurbarán
The Concert
            Hendrik ter Brugghen
The Supper at Emmaus
            Caravaggio
The Virgin in Prayer
            Sassoferratto
Young Woman at a Virginal
            Johannes Vermeer
Still Life with Oranges and Walnuts
            Luis Meléndez

CANDLES

Some local authorities will not licence a production which uses real flame as they consider it to be a fire hazard. Artificial candles are manufactured. Although not as good as the real thing they can be quite effective unless placed too close to the audience.

None of your light sources can be where the candle is on stage, so you will have to use all of your skills to position luminaires carefully.

Depending on where the actors are going to move, some angles will be more open to you than others. If they stay behind the table, low angles from the front or front-side of stage may readily convince us of the correct light source.

As we have seen many times before in our final lighting state we must convince an audience that the supposed light source on stage is doing all the work.

As with much of our work as Designers of Light the technical ability and creative achievement incorporated in our work should be masked by the sheer brilliance of the finished product.

Thus a single candle as an apparent light source encircled by our technical expertise – by modern equipment striving to make it seem real – is a fitting image with which to end this book.

BIBLIOGRAPHY

Beginners' Guides

Fraser, Neil, *Lighting & Sound*, 2nd edn. (Phaidon Press, 1991)

Morgan, Nigel, H., *Stage Lighting for Theatre Designers* (Herbert Press, 1995)

Reid, Francis, *The ABC of Stage Lighting* (A & C Black, 1992)

Reid, Francis, *The Stage Lighting Handbook*, 5th edn. (A & C Black, 1996)

Streader, T., & Williams J., *Create Your Own Stage Lighting* (Bell & Hyman, 1985)

Advanced Guides

Fraser, Neil, Stage Lighting Explained (The Croword Press, 2002)

Pilbrow, Richard, *Stage Lighting Design* (Nick Hern Books, 1997)

Reid, Francis, *Discovering Stage Lighting* (Focal Press, 1993)

Reid, Francis, *Lighting The Stage* (Focal Press, 1995)

Specialized Areas

Rees, Terence, *Theatre Lighting in the Age of Gas* (The Society for Theatre Research, 1978)

Walne, Graham, *Projection for the Performing Arts* (Focal Press, 1997)

Walne, Graham (ed.), *Effects for the Theatre* (A & C Black, 1995)

Associated Subjects

Armstrong, Tim, *Colour Perception* (Tarquin Publications, 1991)

Berger, John, *Ways of Seeing* (BBC & Penguin, 1972)

Brook, Peter, *The Open Space* (Penguin, 1970)

Esslin, Martin, *The Theatre of the Absurd*, rev.edn. (Penguin Books, 1968)

Gaskill, William, *A Sense of Direction* (Faber & Faber, 1988)

Holt, Michael, *Stage Design & Properties* (Phaidon Press, 1988)

Innes, Christopher, *Modern British Drama 1890–1990* (Cambridge University Press, 1992)

Lamb, Trevor & Bourriau, Janine, *Colour Art & Science* (Cambridge University Press, 1995)

Langmuir, Erika, *The National Gallery Companion Guide* (National Gallery Publications, 1994)

Laver, James, *Costume and Fashion* (Thames & Hudson, 1982)

Styan, J.L., *Modern Drama in Theory and Practice*, Vols 1–3 (Cambridge University Press, 1981)

Sudjic, Deyan, *The Lighting Book* (Mitchell Beazley, 1985)

Thorne, Gary, *Stage Design: A Practical Guide* (The Crowood Press, 1999)

INDEX

INDEX